Instant Insanity

Katherine Washburn

authorHOUSE®

AuthorHouse™
1663 Liberty Drive
Bloomington, IN 47403
www.authorhouse.com
Phone: 1 (800) 839-8640

Published by AuthorHouse 11/23/2015

ISBN: 978-1-5049-6304-6 (sc)
ISBN: 978-1-5049-6303-9 (e)

Contents

Instant Insanity

Chapter 1

Dr. Rodriguez

Dreams, have we not had a hundred or more?

Personally, I liked dreams, especially when I had heard that they helped to make-up the person's total being, that saying was over fifty-years ago. My husband and I were both born in June 1942. When I was young, I had heard that if a dream awakens you, it was one of importance. Your subconscious self was telling you something.

Ahhh, dreams could oscillate like a pendulum, viewing good deeds and even evil. Often the reveries themselves would identify who desired the part of playing nice guy and who craved the part of the other. The reverie would baffle and bewilder. The dream could also be used as areas to research in waking life, as did one dream to me.

In the twilight of a December 1978 reverie, I could hear the dream speak the word "Remember." I thought it was I speaking, so I drifted along with the remembrance. In the dream, it was as if I was watching a TV screen. The scene was inside a hospital. A short, dark-haired man wearing a white doctor's coat entered my

room. Quickly, I remembered the 1978 reality scene, when Dr. Rodriguez walked into the room to visit me. I had met Dr. Rodriguez once and that was in July 1978. It was on the second day of my five-day hospitalization. In 1977 the year prior to my hospitalization, I had heard Dr. Rodriguez's name mentioned several times when Carl and son were hospitalized. The doctor expert trinity was Dr. Walker (family doctor), Dr. Rodriguez (internal medicine), and Dr. Evans (surgeon). On the fifth day of my hospitalization, I had met with a phenomenon, a hospital ghost that said; "This is your last ride home!"

It scared the shit out of me. I put my clothes on and went home with my last visitor, which was my husband, Carl. Someone might call the phantom's voice an apparition, a spirit, or a guardian angel. Meanwhile, Carl was angry as he thought that we might have to pay the $2500 hospital bill.

Clearly I remembered Dr. Rodriguez's visit. "Yes, that was in 1978," I replied to the dream.

Then the dream showed a second visit with Dr. Rodriguez. Dr. Rodriguez sat at his medical desk, thinking about Kristine's next medical test. I could clearly hear his thoughts: "If I run a test on the kidneys, then Dr. Evans would run an ovary test."

I had only met Dr. Rodriguez once; there was never a second time. So, I replied: "No, I don't remember that!"

The dream scene darkened, and answered in a slow, firm tone: "Y-o-u-d better!"

There was something in the dream that gave me the impression that the two 1977 surgeries represented two devious-deed items: one was medical greed and the other was the destruction of the United States antibiotic policies.

I felt annoyed and uncomfortable with the dream's words, so I started talking to the dream. "I only saw Dr. Rodriguez once, and that was on the second day of my five-day hospitalization. He never visited me a second time. Why are you telling me that he did?"

The dream's voice replied: "The chemicals can illuminate as well as eliminate."

I woke annoyed with the thoughts that a doctor would deliberately prescribe an ill fate...especially mine. My thoughts reminisced about every word that was mentioned during my one visit with Dr. Rodriguez. The doctor and I briefly discussed Dr. Walker thinking that the problem was in the ovary. Dr. Rodriguez and I also briefly mentioned Carl and son's 1977 surgeries. The next test Dr. Rodriguez ordered was the kidney test.

According to the dream, the dyes used in both the kidney and ovary tests would cause a reaction, and probably fatal. Somehow the dream's symbol reminded me that a lie could destroy a complete country.

In 1978, I had walked out of the hospital because of the unusual voice, appearing and saying: "This is your last ride home!" I knew nothing about chemical reactions.

The following night as I entered the dream world, I could again hear the word "Remember."

I carefully examined the dream scene. This time, I saw my dreamself standing in front of a six-foot tall bookcase. My eyes scanned the blurred book titles. As I looked toward to the top, two books were vivid and it was as if the TV lens had zoomed-in to focus. I'm only five-foot-three, so I couldn't reach the top shelf were the two books stood upright in the shelf middle and were surrounded by many other books. I strained my eyes to read the titles. One had a white cover and the title The Walk Over was printed on the book's spine, while the other had a black cover and sat further inside the bookcase, creating a shadowy outline. I couldn't see the second book's title. It set too far into the darken shadows. The dream then revealed the books complete contents in two words: "My Salvation."

Immediately, I could see my dreamself look more closely for a real title. My eyes scanned the books outline for details. All I could see was that the book was covered in black and sat a little too high for clarity.

Then suddenly "The Walk Over" book fell from the shelf. The 8-1/2"X11" white pages drifted through space. I watched my dreamself read the pages. At first, I was impressed. I could see $250,000 was laced within the falling pages. The dream narrated, "Simple write the book the way you lived it. When it goes upon the shelf, it will go under non-fiction. Mine will be the biggest prophet of them all."

I watched my dream-face-person's facial expression change from impressed to disgust, as I read each page drifting in front of my dreamself eyes. Another panic attack flared. My dreamself stepped back horrified. Raising my hand, I said, "No. It's not enough. No. I'm not going to do that!" I was furious at this remember-thing dream. First, it showed how easily a doctor could kill me; now it was showing the stupidest words I have ever heard.

I turned to exit. As I reached the open doorway, I turned again to face the narrator and have my last say: "Who do you think your are?"

Again, I saw my dreamself's facial expression change, as my dreamself stared at the dream's narrator. The dream itself identified the facial expression. It represented that my dreamself saw God.

The scene again darkened. The darkness changed into a lit movie scene. It was a clear, rapid motion-picture-show to show my life flashing before me, one vision after another. It was similar to a short film clip with the narrator speaking.

The first picture was our six-year-old son standing and facing me with horror in his eyes. The dream explained, "By the time, he's eight, the terror will be there on his face." (Two years later the déjà vu appeared. By the time my son was eight, he had plumed extremely backwards. He didn't even know his birthday date.)

The next picture was a man lying in a hospital bed. The head of the bedstead was elevated and the patient had pillows propping his body into a half-sitting position. My husband Carl and I entered the room. As quickly as we appeared, it was time to depart. Carl stood at the foot of the bed by the door leading to the hospital corridor. I walked back to Sherman, Carl's father to give him a good-bye kiss. (In April 1983, the déjà vu appeared)

The image began to scramble. The scene changed. The dream focused on Carl and me standing near the edge of a different hospital bed. Large medicine cabinets with large plate glass doors stood in the background. The dream presented the diagnosis as "Hodgkin's disease." (In August 1982, the déjà vu appeared, yet it wasn't until May 1983

that Carl's diagnose was Hodgkin's disease; after Carl's blood infection became strong enough to disintegrate bones.)

Again the scene changed. In the center sat a good-like myth figurine. The item sparkled with a golden radiance, increasing its glow by saying: "All of the earth and all of the heavens will be mine."

By the dream's end, I could feel myself lost. I had nowhere to turn and no place to go. So, I reached for the figurine. It was a small object. As my hand touched the figurine, it shattered, releasing millions of sparks in all directions and jolted me awake.

Once I was awake, I noticed that the dream prompted me to ask for medical records.

The first medical record was my 1978 hospitalization. I was shocked to read that Dr. Evans had ordered the Ovary test exactly as the dream had said happened. I complained to the Osteopathic Society that a doctor could use medical tests that could kill and nobody would notice!

Two months prior to the Doctor Rodriguez dream, my brother the table maker made the table that was used in the 1978 Shroud of Turin testing. First brother had placed a bid for the job, and then he was supposed to receive the table back, in place of money.

Well, you know how religious liars are. They are as bad as health saboteurs are. The priest told the United States judge that God wanted him to have it free-for-nothing! So naturally the judge agreed.

I had joined a writer's workshop and shared the medical replies with the members. Also, I designed the book's cover. It was a hand drawn picture on a plastic overlay of the image on the cloth that was known as "The Shroud of Turin" and a photo of brother's table beneath.

At the workshop, three subjects were mentioned: 1) The Bible, 2) The 1950's prescription drug law that made health saboteurs/drug prescribers the official strongest god, 3) My book's cover. My hand drawn cover was called a "nightmare".

The Bible described evildoers and liars. The Bible also stated "For the life of the flesh is in the blood". Yet, blood tests were used to deny my Carl and me the right to the more effective antibiotics/medicines. I have used my husband's 1982 blood test as an example of the importance of establishing a personal blood test figure. It would be like having your personal blood test bible. It would be your way of knowing if you have a medical evildoer and not an honest doctor. When the 1908 tuberculosis vaccine was boycotted, doctors knew it. So, I felt that at the time of the 1978 dream, every doctor knew that the United States prescription drug law was also used to withhold antitumor/antiviral antibiotics.

An example of Carl's 1982 laboratory figures increased would be the following:

Blood Test Patients Lab Figures
(Increased Lab Figures) Personal

WBC	10.9 H	4.8-10.0	(4.8-10.8)	6.0
Myelocytes	0 (a blood-disease indicator)			
Neutrophils	66*	54-62	(45-75)	59
Lymphocytes	26	25-33	(15-45)	30
Monocytes	6	3-7	(0-12)	5
Eosinophils	1 1-3	(0-4)	1	
Basophils	1*	0-0.5	(0-2)	.02*

*Notice the decimal point.

The figures were not flagged because of laboratory increase figures, therefore the cell abnormalities were not noticed, yet Carl's neck tumor was noticeable.

Myelocytes used to be included in the white blood cell differential % figure. Myelocytes were found in the bone marrow and when they appeared in the blood, they were considered a disease marker. Myelocytes and basophils were stained together.

Why would a blood test be important?

The President and his congress that created the prescription drug law; they also created drug over-seers. The government issued drug over-seers were discouraging new antibiotics made from the known mutated new germ cell strains that were discovered in the 1960's. The drug over-seers also knew that hospital laboratories had raised blood test tolerance level figures as much as four (4) times the normal in order to camouflage pathogens that appeared in the blood. A person could not receive any antibiotics unless a drug prescriber gave permission to pay additional money to purchase them. The drug prescriber made more money running medical tests, than truthfully reading blood tests and prescribing antibiotics!

Several medical specialists were telling people that blood did not feed the tissue.

The action was saying that the Bible statement lied "For the life of the flesh is in the blood", and the Bible also called a liar "A liar". Medical evildoers have existed since the Biblical times.

Since we live with many subjects appearing at the same time, I tried to remember every detail about my mother's sister Mia who died of Hodgkin's disease in 1970. Aunt Mia was bitter about her unnecessary surgeries. She also had undergone a great deal of radiation and pain before death. In 1970, her body was donated to the National Cancer Society. Public knowledge increased available information. About 1914, it was believed that a gram-negative bacterial-infection caused Hodgkin's disease.

When I compared the Antibiotic Era (1940-1960), with the newer antibiotics that were made from mutated germs, it stopped with Adriamycin. The anti-tumor/anti-viral antibiotics were available in the 1960's, but Aunt Mia's doctors didn't prescribe. They favored surgery and radiation. When the drug prescribers didn't prescriber certain antibiotics, the manufacturers would have no reason to produce them. I believe that was where the smart germ cliché was created: "A brainless bacterium is smarter than a human with a brain."

The United States (US) prescription drug law didn't fall from the sky; the Congress during the Korean War (1950-1953) passed it. Many people living in the US don't know where or how the "Caution: Federal law prohibits the dispensing without prescription" law came to exist. I believe that there should be a day to commemorate.

That way the US people would know who passed the law and how the law was designed to safeguard the US people or the Health Saboteurs.

The law deprives me my right to the better antibiotics, such as Adriamycin, Bleomycin, and Streptomycin. Many people have told me to go to another country for the antibiotic drugs. I felt that writing my congress people and requesting the right to the better antibiotics, and not the over-used ones, would be the better way.

I believe that only in America (USA) would lawmakers legalize Health Sabotage. Yes, I believe that Health Saboteurs were in the United States during WW1.

A century ago the #1 disease killer was tuberculosis (TB), thus TB vaccines were sought after and discovered, but not in the USA. When the 1908 TB vaccine was discovered, it was used throughout the world, except in the USA. I thought that was unusual, until my husband had a neck tumor in 1982. Doctors made more money by treating with inferior drugs and they received great recognition by discovering new diseases. So some doctors were withholding the 1960's discovered anti-tumor antibiotics in order to create new diseases. Carl's hematologist called his Hodgkin's disease "Castleman-Iverson disease" and didn't use antibiotics until after using blood transfusions. The blood transfusions that contained special antibodies left enough infection to disintegrate bones (1983). I had Carl change doctors and hospitals in order to survive.

Needless to say, several medical people told Carl that the patient does NOT question the doctor or ask for the better antibiotics, and that the patient doesn't need any medical records.

I think it's disgusting that a medical society would recommend treatment plans that were deadlier than the disease and a legal society that would support what should have been called "Health Sabotage".

Instant Insanity

Chapter 2

The Conference Dream (1978)

The following dream that I titled "The Conference Dream" introduced educational, medical, and psychological lies that were already embedded. The dream contained the second reason that Dr. Rodriguez would kill to cover-up medical lies, and it also forewarned a death.

A few months after "The Conference Dream", I met the woman who had appeared in the dream. Her name was Dorothy Carter. Her son was one of my son's classmates named Donald. Dorothy's hair was sandy-brown and she worn it short, a becoming style caressing her face. A faint, two-inch scar made her right cheek noticeable. I remembered meeting her, but I couldn't remember from where. As Dorothy spoke, I also recognized her voice.

"I've met you someplace," I awkwardly said, while trying to figure out where we had met. "It must have been at the school. Seems like I remember talking to you."

"No," Dorothy answered, "it wasn't me you met."

I persisted, "I'm not very good on names, but I remember faces. Yes, I've met you someplace."

"No," Dorothy insisted, "it wasn't me you met. I'm not very good on names, but I do remember faces. No! I've never seen you before in my life!"

I erased the conversation from my mind and enjoyed Donald's birthday party. Then I remember where I had met Dorothy. She was the woman in the conference dream.

In the dream, I could see myself standing outside a big blue door. My feelings were tense and I hesitated to enter. I was new to this area and unfamiliar with the way things were done. The dream's aura was filled with information making it clear that the speaker's words would be a well-written fictional speech. The prose would describe a convincing phenomenon that the speaker, himself personally had seen and known to be totally untrue.

To my surprise, my tall, slender neighbor, Betty was to enter the school building and would be walking straight for the conference room that was on the other side of the blue door by which I stood. Before Betty opened the door to enter, I already knew that her words would not be factual, either. I asked of my neighbor, "Betty, why are you here at this conference?"

"I'm a nurse," said Betty who was wearing a white turtleneck and a comfortable plaid A-shaped shirt. Betty nonchalantly threw her arms in the air, continuing with her explanation, "and they want medical expertise. Free advice is better than no advice at all."

My thoughts flowed from my mouth, "Wouldn't the word 'expert' come under the word 'doctor' and not a nurse who passes out at the sight of blood?"

Betty didn't answer. She proceeded to open the door and enter the conference room in her usual bubbly athlete manner. I followed my neighbor inside.

I sat next to Betty, who took the chair at the right corner of the long, polished wood-grain conference table. As I looked at all the people occupying the chairs on both sides, I was amazed that I knew most of them. I didn't know the woman who was sitting directly across from me. This conference was taking place for her benefit. I could see my dreamself staring at the woman. Her hair was sandy brown and worn in a short, becoming style caressing her face. A faint, two-inch scar made her right cheek noticeable. On the sandy-haired woman's left and sitting across from Betty was a tall, blonde pre-school educator. To my extreme left and at the head of the long table sat the school's principal, Mr. Daniels, a heavy-set man dressed in a distinct gray suit. The chair directly across the table's length was being saved for the sociologist, who would be arriving shortly.

The conference began. To me, the discussion was to deliberately confuse reality by incorporating lies. The false words were used to scatter common-sense truth into an unrelated language. Finally almost everybody (myself excluded) nodded and agreed that

the topic of giving human sacrifice to a mythical god was understandable and positively presented! I found the agreement provoking.

In the dream, I could see my dreamself tilting my head down, searching for something to say against the human sacrifice. A piece of paper appeared filled with notes. It was only one paper. I didn't know much about the subject, but somehow I knew there were seventy years of living example embodied in this paper. Yet, for this conference that wasn't enough information. The giving of human sacrifice to a lying god angered me. In a stage of bewilderment, I spoke anyway: "I can't agree with you," I said voicing the only opposition to the ungodly sacrifice. "This information you are offering is leaving something out! The word death is replacing the word life. The realm in which we walk: two-out-of-five are successfully dead; one-out-of-five is left very much deranged; then the remaining two-out-of five seem to disappear, and nobody thinks it's noteworthy, nor do they follow-up on the recommendation.

"What information are you offering? Only the reaching for straws when you already know better yourself! There are four of us sitting here who are referred to as 'the only ones.' Well, if I'm going to be the only one, it will be just as it is said 'the only one!'"

The statistics that I was quoting were based on the results of the misleading and misguiding information. The false information was encouragement to suicide among the young. The figure of two-out-of-five children never reaching adulthood, I thought was quite high.

I then pointed to the woman with the sandy brown hair, continuing, "I'd be asking, 'Who's dead?' She'll be the fifth entering this realm. Shall we call it a step into the dark side of humanity? If she cannot find her answers from within, she's never going to find them; but should she run out of words while deciding not to promenade around this sphere in which we gather, I'd be the first to defend her. I would pull out my knives, hoping to alter the tides and turn the winds, changing the character to no other shade than the color that he is!"

The principal, Mr. Daniels, spoke, "All this is very fine. Someday, maybe these facts could be helpful. Unfortunately, they're of no use now. They mean nothing. You see only the fourth. You're not looking at the three before. Wait. Wait until your eyes are open, and you're not so blind. The trial is your own!"

"My trial!" I raised my voice in a rage. "What are you saying? You're closing your eyes to everything that is mentioned!" All of a sudden, a large club appeared in my right hand. I began showing the club and waving it like a weapon in a threatening manner. "You see this club?

"I'm going to use it; I don't care what it does, or whom it hits! At least it will be far more honest than anything else has been! You walk in this realm in which the deed is sought. Yet, you do not speak in the manner that you yourself have been taught. You tell of everything-everything that's naught! You're blinder than I am. If you think that I cannot see, simply open your eyes. Watch, as I show you exactly what I mean!"

IrRitated and violent at the nonsense, I swung the club. Everyone in the room watched it encircle the table with rage. As the weapon completed its journey to encircle all observers, two heads were chopped off at the end of the motion, the school principal and the unknown woman. I, too, was shocked and looked in amazement at the item clutched in my hand. It was no longer a club; it had turned into an axe! I wasn't that angry with the principal, and I didn't know the woman with the short sandy-brown hair at all. The conference was for her. It was she whom we were helping.

Several people had disappeared. There were only three of us left in the conference scene: the two that I had just beheaded and me. Since everybody else was gone, I thought that the conference was over. I stood up to leave. As I proceeded to walk away, the long-awaited sociologist was sitting at the corner of the table. His image was unclear, but his masculine voice calmly spoke, "We understand."
End of Dream

I woke bewildered and wondering how the woman whom the conference was supposed to help came into the way of the axe? What concerned me the most was that the dream clearly had presented that both the medical and the educational society gave out false and misleading information that encouraged the psychological affect that resulted in juvenile suicide!

Time had passed and I had been on two kindergarten's zoo trip. One trip was with my son's room and the other with my daughter, which was where I received the story idea for a child's book titled "Lost at the Zoo".

The dream prompted my looking closer at all medical and educational advice, even when it was from my neighbor, Betty. Soon I found myself arguing with Betty and my husband Carl over education. Carl would shake his head and make light of both Betty and me by saying, "One thinks that they're right and the other knows that they're right. Both of you have become arguing idiots."

When I was in Duane's first grade classroom, the teacher and I spoke. As we conversed, I found it difficult to understand what was being said. The teacher's favorite words were "Child Conscious". Every time the teacher spoke "Child Conscious" the walls would turn bloody red, as if to say that the words didn't match the action. I withdrew from argument as I could feel my body be overcome with nausea and sweat. The perspiration turned to chills as I looked to the left wall, which read: "If feelings were blood, the walls are red!"

In reality, I was speechless, and left the room until our next meeting, which was a conference. Several teachers and the schools principal, Mr. Daniels was there. Sitting next to me was a Mrs. Perez, who had tested my son Duane and felt that the testing showed him to be dyslexic. The teacher was shocked that 8-year-old Duane didn't know his birthday date. I looked at Mrs. Barn's short sandy brown hair, as she spoke of everything, except the meaning of the tests.

"Ducks!" Mr. Daniels was astonished. He shook his head, and snapped at the chance for a better explanation of the remark. "What do ducks have to do with this conference?"

I shrugged my shoulders, answering, "They tell about flying, normal reactions, senses, inner instincts, the pecking order, the will to survive, nature, and even godliness."

The conference ended. I returned home to write down all the ducks had taught up to that point of time, and the realities of keeping back a dyslexic. According to the dream, there was no advantage when a negative was being coordinated with a lie. It was obvious that the principal and I were having difficulty communicating. Finally I told him about son's February 1977 un-descended testis surgery. The principal then told me about his boy who at the age of six had the same surgery.

Immediately, I thought of the age. At age six, the surgery would have been unsuccessful. Our family doctor recommended that the surgery be done before age five; otherwise it was unsuccessful. I believed the Dr. Walker because the problem was on both sides of the families. No one in either family had any health problem resulting from the malformation, yet there was an uncle was not able to join the military or join in any sports because of it. In the early 1970's the malformation involved 15% of school

age males. The educational and psychological mode was obviously the biggest problem. I contacted the military to confirm what had happened to the uncle who tried to join. I thought that I had researched the subject quite well, before making the decision and talking my husband into agreeing to Duane's 1977 surgery.

After fumbling for a few words, I said, "Age six is too old to be successful."

The word "unsuccessful" moved slowly around the room, until the principal said, "I thought I was the only one." Mr. Daniels then changed the subject to explain how removing the testis removed a possible future cancer problem.

"That wasn't our case," I replied. "The body will dissolve the problem. Unknowing, we took our screaming child into an unnecessary surgery. They did a kidney test after to use the excuse that maybe the kidneys were underdeveloped, too. Had they had done a test to check prior to the surgery, the kidney test after would have killed him!"

I was under the impression that the principal's son was older than mine was. It had taken many years before the recommended surgery was changed from age 6 to 5. The people in the educational, medical, or psychological societies never mentioned the unsuccessful surgeries, deaths, and suicide figures. As for preventing a future cancer, if a person chopped off their head, brain cancer would be eliminated!

Our conversation was going in two different directions. So, I ended our chat with "Some is going to die!" There was a living-aura from scribbled title "Ducks Teach Me How to Raise My Children" story that swirled around the room, saying, "For words that go unsaid and deed which go undone, survival is being neglected and someone is about to die!"

Mr. Daniels stated, "No way could, or would, this school be involved in anything such as a death," he paused to change the subject to the duck story: "It's all so superimposed! Sometimes one's imagination can escape realities, especially if that someone is bored, misguided, or frustrated." Mr. Daniels then said, holding up the duck story, "This comes from years of depression."

I didn't think that that was my problem, especially when the principal had a child himself with the same problem. Thus I left the principal's office with a cover idea. My book titled "The Walk-Over" cover design. It would have two pictures; one picture would be hand-drawn on a plastic over-lay, covering a photo.

Mr. Daniels and I were surprised and shocked when two-and-a-half-weeks later, Donald was run over and killed by one of Lake Orion's school buses.

I was at the zoo with Donald and my boy the year before I was at the zoo with my daughter Miley. I wrote the story "Lost at the Zoo" and used Miley's Zoo trip in place of the one Donald had gone on because it was much more interesting. I wanted to speak with Donald's mother. Between the dreams, the walls turning blood red and Donald's death, the situation bothered me. I took the children book with me to visit Dorothy. I told her about the phenomenon. Dorothy wasn't surprised at hearing it. A few months prior to Donald's being killed by the school bus, she and Donald had gone to a palmist. Donald's palm had shown a short life expectancy.

The subject returned to my son's schoolwork. My husband, too, was at son's next school conference. The subject again was retainment. Carl agreed to keep son back, if he didn't perform. My English was (and still is) very poor. Anyway, after the conference, I re-wrote the "Ducks Teach Me How to Raise My Children", and returned to the principal's office. I questioned the educational philosophy about educating a child who was brought into an unnecessary surgery screaming. The principal and I ended our meeting with my saying, "If you wish to keep my son back, then prepare yourself to take me to court!"

The "Conference Dream" talked about lies, and how medical and educational lies would encourage suicide among the young. At the time the realities were saturated with lies, and it was obvious that a doctor would kill before additional questions could be asked. I began interpreting the dream and looking for the 70-years of research page.

DREAM DESCRIPTION: Before entering the conference room, the dream describes the scene as one of thievery. Thievery: The practice or act of thieving; theft. Thief: one who steals. Someone who takes something that belongs to another. The dream describes the thievery as 4-fold. Two deceptions (educational and medical) were clearly identified before entering the room.

BUILDING: The construction was built of lies. I'm inside the building whether I want to be there or not. Personally, I didn't believe that a person could build their life based on lies, but the people in the dream were showing me that it could be done. It would be extremely complicated to live a life based on lies. Think about the number of lies. To justify the spiritual aspect would mean to distort the scientific facts. A redefinition of common word usage would be an easy way of confusion and contradiction. The lie comes from the Earth gods by making political laws to justify a misdoing. "What is suppose to be," and "the reality of what is" are two different entities. The dreamer would have to research reality as opposed to nonexistence reality. The building usually represented self.

MY CONCLUSION: I'm a realist, and to me the building of a life based on a lie would be a dangerous thing. The dream represented Past, Present, and Future. The woman in the dream was like myself staring into a mirror glass that would represent my dreamself. The woman must have spoke, but her words were garble and I couldn't understand them. Then when I tried to place my finger on a clear subject, the educational image as well as the medical text facts and truths would be misleading or misrepresented.

CLUB: You will undergo a rough and profitless journey. The club had an identity; it was to beat down a lie. Yes, the club had turned into a sharp blade, which gave the item several definitions. One interesting interpretation was the separation and quarrels and losses in affairs of a business character.

CROWD: If people are handsomely dressed, it denotes pleasant associations. But if marred, it will denote distress and unhappiness where profit and congenial intercourse was expected.

70 years of Research Words:

In 1900 when tuberculosis was the #1 disease killer, doctors did NOT wish that United States taxpayers money spent on looking for a tuberculosis vaccine. I'll see you and your siblings sick before I see you receive the 1908 BCG vaccine to fight the #1 disease killer tuberculosis family bacteria. They wanted the taxpayer money to be spent on disease studies and the buildings where the tuberculosis patients were treated. The Tetanus vaccine had already been discovered. The Bible trinity was known as Father (God), Son, and Holy Spirit, while the prescription drug law created a legalized drug lord. The Bible gave several blood references, one of which says, "For the life of the flesh is in the blood." Meanwhile, it was also know that pathogens used the blood as a vessel to travel to various body parts.

The evil doctors used government-funded money to treat (but not cure) and to study the bacterial damage done to the human body by the various tuberculosis bacteria-family germs. The prescription drug law would form a new trinity using them as the god-figure, health saboteur, and anti-Christ. They would promote the opposite of "For the life of the flesh is in the blood" by saying, "Suck the blood from the flesh; blood means nothing!" (Biopsies are tissue only!)

I thought it strange that Medicare would not ask for paid-for blood tests to be received tests upon payment. A blood test would be like the patient's personal health bible. The patient must establish his or her personal blood references. I assumed that people remembered Nikita Khrushchev famous prediction that the United States would perish from within. He must have known more about the evil doctors than the people. I also assumed that people knew that the bacterial-produced tuberculosis disease was the #1 disease killer in the United States for over a century when the United States prescription drug law was passed. Taxpayer money was spent to study the tuberculosis (TB) disease, but never a penny was spent looking for a vaccine. Other countries were also looking for a TB vaccine and one was discovered.

An old tuberculosis vaccine writing as the following:

B.C.G. Vaccine: a vaccine introduced in France about 1908 by Bacillus Calmette and Guerin. The Calmette-Guerin bacillus used is a live attenuated strain of the Mycobacterium tuberculosis. It may be given to infants who are especially exposed to the risk of tuberculous infection and to young people who are shown by the tuberculin test to have no natural immunity to the disease. It may be given to all medical students, veterinary students and nurses who have no natural immunity and come into contact with tuberculosis. It is not used in the United States because chemical means of prevention are considered more effective and do not interfere with the skin test used in epidemiology and private practice as a single means to test incidence of infection in the population.

End of 1908 tuberculosis vaccine's write-up.

To me, "private practice meant that the medical society wished for a larger business. The evil doctor wished for the prescription drug law. It would enable more United States money flowing for more tuberculosis disease studies, while nothing would be spent looking for a sensible cure. Then the evil doctor moved to destroy the United States antibiotic policies. A health saboteur could do more damage to people than any terrorist. The dream had added thoughts about comparing the antibiotics that were available after World War 2 with the antibiotics and vaccines that would be used going into another war. The United States scientists knew in the 1950's that all cells mutated and that antibiotics could be made from the mutated germ cells. I wished to have access to the antitumor/antiviral antibiotics.

As I researched reality, I was shocked to discover that I lived in a state where the prescription drug law was used to deprive my husband and me the right to the more effective gram-negative antibiotics, medicines, and to honest medical advice!

Instant Insanity

Chapter 3

Rebuttals

I'd notice that dreams incorporate several subjects. Each subject should be carefully examined. The suicide statistics that the educational and medical societies were covering up bothered me.

The woman in the conference dream ended up with a dead child in reality, while I had a Duane-can't-spell dilemma. Duane's teacher was telling Duane that it was all right to learn only half the spelling words, and then telling us that it was NOT all right. Throughout my life, children were used as pawns by the educational system to increase taxes, most of which was for salary increases. How using a child as a schooling tax pawn influenced juvenile suicide was never mentioned!

Meanwhile, germs and parasites were also a big problem. When Duane was in second grade and his sister Miley was in first grade, Duane said, "Mom, I've got bugs in my hair".

My first thought was head lice. I asked, "How could you tell"?

"I scratched my head, and a bug was under my fingernail".

I looked at Duane's head and saw another louse. I remembered when I was in the first grade. The school nurse checked regularly for head lice, it was a common problem. Mother had washed my hair with kerosene or gasoline; I couldn't remember which one. So I decided that I would drive to the local store to purchased head lice shampoo. I returned home to wash heads, bedding and the next day reported the head lice to the school.

Shortly after, a second head lice problem was again present. By this time there was no over-the-counter-head-lice-shampoo at any local store. So, I went to the doctor's to have him write a prescription head lice shampoo, and again reported the problem to the school.

The head lice problem had affected both the first and second grade to an epidemic problem. Finally, the school decided to inform the parents. The school called me, stating that they had a head lice problem and they were sending the infested children home. They had sent a total of four children home from the first and second grade, two of which were mine.

I drove Duane and Miley to the Health Department for head lice shampoo and a note from the Health Department person so that both children could return to the Un-Child Conscious School.

By the time Duane was eight, he didn't know his birthday date. I wondered if that teacher's statement was another school rebuttal? Between the unnecessary surgery and what I felt was an unnecessary head lice epidemic, I told the school principal, "You wish to keep my son back then you can take me to court!"

Duane was placed in the third grade labeled dyslexic for a better specialize education. It was a constant No-Win situation. At the time, the most common pier phrase was "You're in special education because you're stupid."

Instant Insanity

Chapter 4

Stupid Toes

A friend named Leo asked me to accompany her on a visit to a Hospital. Leo had been sick and wanted a second opinion. She thought I might help her navigate since I had taken many-wrong-turns for the 60-mile drive to my husband's Hospital near by.

Leo had gone to the Internet for directions. It gave the quickest route as M-59 to US-23 exit 39 as 47-miles and the estimated arrival time (EAT) was 64 minutes. She picked me up at 8:30 a.m., which gave us two hours to be at the hospital for her 10:30 a.m. appointment. I had never driven that way, so I was trying to take memory notes, as a good navigator should.

We were driving down US-23 when I noticed exit 45. The rain drops began splattering on the windshield. It began pouring, and the car window-wipers wouldn't work. My friend had to pull off the road and wait for the rain to stop. Leo recently had her car worked on. She told the car dealership that the wipers didn't properly work; they had a pause wiping when it rained. It was clear that the $400 she spent at the dealership to repair her car didn't include the wipers. As the windows began to fog and the sound of thunder surrounded us, we sat helplessly as the traffic sped by uncomfortably close drenching the car and our thoughts.

I looked down at Leo's large manila folders that contained her medical records. I could see her brain scan folder. I had gone with her for that test, too.

My friend then mentioned that she couldn't afford a copy of her bone marrow test. The doctor wanted $65 for a copy, if she wished to take it with her.

We briefly discussed the outrageous prices that were charged for copies of paid-for medical test reports. I also didn't see Leo's 1994 breast-tumor biopsy or her 1994 blood tests. My friend had gone to the same hospital that had raised the laboratory blood-test-high-tolerance-level figure 10 times the normal figure (.01-5.0%) that a person in Lansing stated the figure should have been (0-.5%). I immediately associated bacterial produced neurological disorders with the ulcer problem. It took 50 years before a doctor stated bacteria caused many ulcers. Therefore, there may be more Ronald White druggists/doctors in the United States than realized. So what would a modern-day medical Ronald White do? He would wish that the United States antibiotic policies be rendered useless, and maybe even filled with non-cures.

The subject changed as Leo and I looked at the car clock 10:15 time. Leo asked, "Whom should I call? I probably have enough cell battery for one call."

I shrugged my shoulders, and stuttered a reply, "I don't have the slightest idea, but I would place the hospital at the bottom of the list. I'll get out and try giving the wipers a push." I got out to manually move the wipers. It was one push, one wipe. I noticed a piece of black metal was lying by the windshield. The underside was corroded with white mineral deposits. It must have broken off the wiper arm. The black wiper arm had a white spot that was also filled with white mineral deposits. I scrapped the white corrosion with my fingernail. Again the wipers would work only once. So, I returned inside the car.

Leo called the operator. The operator connected her to the police. I, being the navigator, had thought that we were on US-23 between exit 44 and 45. Then as Leo was telling the officer where we were, her cell phone went dead.

At that moment, across the highway, we saw a police car pulling over a motorist. Perhaps it was our guardian angel or just another man's misfortune that brought the police to pull over a motorist directly across the highway.

The officer gave no signs of noticing us. He appeared oblivious to our situation. I jumped out of the car, dashed to the front, and began jumping and waving my arms to draw his attention. It did.

We waited for the officer to finish with the motorist. The rain began letting up. Leo looked at the 10:30 clock and asked, "Do you think he would escort us?"

The officer pulled up behind us and walked over to my window. I explained our situation and asked for an escort. It was a negative, but he told us the hospital exit from M-14.

Shortly, Leo and I arrived at the large hospital complex and immediately parked in the first covered parking lot we approached. It would be easier for us to walk to the appointment.

Once inside the hospital, Leo and I asked numerous people the directions to the test office. Each person had a different perspective of where it was located.

Each person seemed to be allotted only a portion of the puzzle to guide us. Finally we arrived and Leo didn't have a hospital card. The test office was supposed to have all the needed information, but they didn't. So we had to walk to the Card Making Office. We followed the hospital puzzle until finally Leo was called for her test.

I walked around the lobby where four flutists were entertaining from noon to 1 p.m. I had a camera and I wanted to take Leo's picture with the flutists. I returned to the test waiting room disappointed that my friend's test wasn't completed before the flutists left. While I waited, I shut my eyes and drifted into deep thought. Leo's test was completed at 1:15. She walked over to me saying, "You're napping!"

We waited for the test results. When they were ready, Leo asked me to accompany her to take notes.

A white-haired man and a younger woman wearing white jackets entered the room. I assumed that they both were doctors. A quick introduction was made, and I discovered that I couldn't spell their names let alone the medical terms that they were using. The last test was something I had never heard of...the "smart toe test".

Leo didn't pass, and the doctor announced right there in front of his assistance, God, and myself that my friend had stupid toes! There was no treatment for stupid toes. But the doctor said four things that Leo should keep an eye on. 1) Repeat MRI to check on the white matter that appeared on the brain. 2) Check red blood cells concerning a lack of vitamin B12. 3) Rheumatologist panels. 4) It would have been nice to see the bone marrow test. (I, again, thought that it was sad that a doctor would want $65 in order that another doctor could see the test.

While I was at the U of M, I wanted to get the Bacillus Calmette-Guerin (BCG) tuberculosis vaccine. I stopped at the information deck. The lady told me to go to the Department of Internal Medicine. I did. The lady who made the appointment mentioned that my insurance company probably wouldn't pay for the vaccine. I replied, "That's okay. I still want the tuberculosis vaccine."

She then told me that I would need a passport and they would decide if the vaccine was necessary.

Leo and I left the U of M hospital, debating whether to take US-23 or not. If it rained, the traffic would be extremely heavy and with no place to pull off. It wasn't raining, so we took US-23. It started to rain, and Leo took the first exit off the busy highway. Neither of us knew where we were. Then the wipers began to work, so Leo drove back onto the highway.

Leo asked, "What exit do I take to M-59?"

I forgot to write the exit number down, so I took a guess: "60".

We made our exit to M-59 and the wipers stopped again. Leo and I had to stop several times and wait for the pouring rain to let up. Then we would laugh as I got out to manually work the wipers. We made it home literally between raindrops and remained friends.

What was the lesson from this journey? If you want me to be your navigator - you must have smart toes.

The Walk-Over
Chapter 5b

Betty's Invisible Medical Book

Four years had passed since the dream where I had borrowed Ann's diagramed-medical book on March 1, 1979. On March 1, 1983, I had changed my mind about rehashing the symptoms showed in the special-diagram book with my know-it-all neighbor with the so-he's-going-to-die attitude. It upset me to know that if the drug prescriber chose not to prescribe effective antibiotics, the prescription drug law permitted it.

On March 1, 1983, I called Betty to borrow her diagramed-medical book again. The book's Hodgkin's disease description was now appearing in reality, and the doctors (who were specialists) were having problems identifying Carl's illness.

My husband had a neck tumor biopsy done on March 1, 1983, which was the following: "In some areas, especially around foci of necrosis, Reed-Sternberg-like cells are noted. These probably represent binucleate immunoblasts and are not true Reed-Sternberg cells."

(End of biopsy)

I was under the impression that cells, pathogens, and people all have one thing in common - they gathered in families, and they had siblings and mutated. In the 1960's it was known that new antibiotics could be made from the new strains. An example would be Doxorubicin. Somehow this same information could be distorted, and bacterial infections could go unnoticed. Carl had all the symptoms of Hodgkin's disease; yet, the hematologist/drug prescriber wouldn't give the most effective known antibiotics, claiming that the known Hodgkin's disease cell wasn't a perfect match.

On March 1, 1983, it was known that disease studies have been taking placed for centuries. The Hematologist gave me the impression that she needed every one of the disease symptoms before giving an antitumor antibiotic to Carl to treat his neck tumor. Betty quickly came over with every medical book that she owned. So, Betty, Carl, and I quickly rehashed the hematologist care that was given.

For nine months between 1982 and 1983, Carl was under the healthcare of a

hematologist named Dr. McClarens, treating his grapefruit size neck tumor. The hematologist would use Carl as her guinea pig, explaining to her trainees that "soft tumors" were always benign. At the same time, TV had a cancer series, talking about malignant "soft tumors".

In 1982-1983 were three diseases with the same symptoms. They were Castleman-Iverson (an autoimmune deficiency disease without the syndrome), autoimmune deficiency syndrome, and Hodgkin's disease that had the same symptoms. The symptoms were a messed up blood profile, night sweats, and a tumor would often appear on the neck, chest or groin.

Carl asked the hematologist if he had Hodgkin's disease, the reply was "No". Then he asked if he had AIDS. The hematologist laughed, saying that only the gays got that!

My husband and I watched the cancer situation from his patient's point of view. The hematologist wouldn't inform Carl about several blood abnormalities. Therefore, we were not aware that many abnormal blood tests results were used as "markers" to aid in identifying pathogen-produced cancerous conditions. Also that antitumor/antiviral antibiotic like Adriamycin and Bleomycin were no longer administered until infections turned human tissue malignant. Antibiotics attack the pathogen; they don't know the difference between malignant and benign. The drug prescriber determined the difference. It was obvious that the biopsies were for "Tissue only" and the blood pathogens disregarded! Therefore, it was very important that the patient establish his/her personal bible blood test figure.

Carl's 1982 differential blood test was the following:

Blood Test Patients Lab Figures
(Increased Lab Figures) Personal Bible

WBC	10.9 H	4.8-10.0	4.8-10.8	6.0
Myelocytes	0 (a blood-disease indicator)			
Neutrophils	66*	54-62	45-75	59*
Lymphocytes	26	25-33	15-45	30
Monocytes	6	3-7	0-12	5
Eosinophils	1	1-3	0-4	1
Basophils	1*	0-0.5	0-2	.02*

*The Basophils figures were not flagged because of laboratories increased figures; therefore the cell abnormalities were not noticed. And again Carl received no antibiotics.

Myelocytes used to be included in the white blood cell differential % figure. Myelocytes were found in the bone marrow and when they appeared in the blood, they were considered a disease marker. Myelocytes and basophils were stained together. Therefore the philosophy of "Closed eyes do not see," could be also used with the white blood cell staining. There was more money to be made treating a disease than using an antibiotic was what the hematologist was obviously doing. I called the withholding of antitumor antibiotics and the lying about it, "health sabotage a US enemy's delight".

Meanwhile, after months of being treated for an autoimmune deficiency blood disorder, it was recommended by the Henry Ford Hospital specialist that Carl have a modified radical neck surgery to biopsy the neck lymph node tissue. The March 1, 1983 biopsy tissue was sent to three hospitals.

Two hospital biopsy specialists stated the tissue as benign, while the third hospital experts called the tissue Hodgkin's disease/mixed cellularity.

In 1983, it was said that a tumor could be caused by a blood pathogen. In Carl's case, the infection may have seeped into the blood by way of his gums. The hematologist treatment was based on how the infection affected the tissue. Benign tissue received no antibiotics, where malignant tissue would have.

My husband, Carl, would ask the hematologist questions, especially about Hodgkin's disease. She would insist that the disease wasn't Hodgkin's disease. Hodgkin's disease, too, was a known blood disorder. The hematologist used blood transfusions to treat Carl's neck tumor that also had a blood disorder. The transfused blood was checked. Therefore Carl received a Blood Type Identification card that identified special antibodies that had to be identified before he was transfused in the future. In 1983, the Blood

Type Identification tests were an established antibody blood test.

Carl's blood type was:

A2, DCcEe, +DAT, S-, s+, K+k+, Fy a+, Fy b+, Jk a+, Jk b+, which

represented Carl's blood as "A" blood group with special antibodies from

the MNSs, Kell, Duffy, and Kidd groups.

Disease studies have been taking place for centuries. At the time of the older studies, pathogens such as bacteria, fungus, and mold were believed to cause disease. The new studies have eliminated the pathogen affects on the blood. Pathogens would often use the blood as a vehicle. By omitting, the pathogens present in the blood, the tissue damage and symptoms would vary, creating new diseases. When a new disease was discovered, the disease could be named after the doctor or scientist who made the discovery. Indeed a discoverer's feather (a prize), which would be a notable medical recognition.

Carl's disease remained labeled autoimmune deficiency by the hematologist; yet, it appeared as if the hematologist had quit looking for a new disease. The adding of chemicals would also have produced new disease strains. The four-year-old dream clearly presented Carl's health problem as Hodgkin's disease. The complications as to why the health problem was difficult to identify were now appearing, and extremely complicated, simply because of the withholding of antitumor antibiotics when a tumor was clearly seen!

After the hematologist used blood transfusions, in place of antibiotics, her patient's (my husband) illness dramatically worsened. The blood was checked for special antibodies prior to transfusion, which caused me to believe that the withholding of antitumor/antiviral antibiotics created fatal diseases. The medical society had placed the odds of surviving fourth-stage Hodgkin's disease as "always fatal"; and it was said that the established 1983 Blood-Type-Identification test didn't exist, because blood was not checked prior to transfusion. Also there was no attorney who had a doctor available to state that antitumor/antiviral antibiotics were deliberately being withheld. Therefore, Carl's inferior treatment would go unnoticed and unquestioned.

The month after Carl's March 1983 neck biopsy and the special antibody blood transfusions, an infection strong enough to disintegrate bones attacked his back. The hematologist prescribed muscle relaxers. Within a month the pain was back, so the hematologist had Carl hospitalized for therapy.

At the hospital, Carl had what appeared as a compression fracture with an infection disintegrating his spine, spots on his lungs, and enlarged lymph nodes under one arm. Therefore, a second biopsy in May 1983 was recommended. Again, the hematologist insisted that Carl's condition was not Hodgkin's disease. I questioned the hematologist diagnosis. The hematologist raised her arms and stretched them apart to show the mammoth improbability, stating: "For this to be Hodgkin's disease, Carl would have to have had so much chemotherapy and so much radiation that there's no way he could be in this shape with the treatments he's had."

If the disease was Hodgkin's, the hematologist's patient was in the fourth stage and approximately one month from dying! It was obvious that the hematologist was leaving Carl die. While watching the death process, I had God breathing down my neck asking, "Are you going to let the doctor murder your husband?"

So, I asked, "Does this hospital do cancer treatments?"

The reply was "No!" And it was said that the hematologist's last patient was moved to the graveyard on the roof!

So, I went home to call the hospital doctors who had recommended that Carl have the March biopsy.

On May 24, 1983, I called the hematology department to find out what had happened to Dr. McClarens's Castleman-Iverson's new disease diagnosis. Dr. Garcia answered the phone. Dr. Garcia's reply was a question: "Are you looking for litigation?"

There was a deadly health problem. I had felt that his remark was totally unnecessary, and certainly out-of-place. Again, my husband had gone into the hospital on May 13, 1983. Carl had an enlarged lymph node under his right arm, spots on his lungs, and a compression fracture that was more than a fracture - with the fracture was an infection that was disintegrating his spine daily.

Dr. Garcia transferred me to Dr. King. Again, I explained that Carl had a compression fracture and an infection that was moving down his spine daily. Dr. King informed that after the March 1, 1983 neck biopsy, the laboratory diagnosed Carl's condition as Hodgkin's disease (mixed cellularity). Apparently Dr. McClarens also sent tissue samples to Lukes in Florida and Betty Arbor. After Dr. McClarens received the two reports as benign, she condensed the reports into one letter to Dr. King. The doctor was not aware of any complications.

For Carl to go to the hospital now for treatment, they would have to do the back biopsy before they could treat him.

On May 25, 1983 at 8:40 a.m., Carl was wheeled to surgery. It took two surgeons to perform what I was told was a "Laminectomy", while Carl was told that it was a "Thoracotmy". Dr. Mitri opened the chest cavity to move the lungs and other organs, while Dr. Shannon scrapped as much of the green moss and abscess from the infected inside-back area. The spinal cord 5-6-7 thoracic area was infected with an abscess. The purpose was to drain the abscess for biopsy and cultural purposes.

At 1:10 p.m. both doctors came to the waiting room. A section of rib was removed and placed in the back where one vertebrae was so infected that moss appearing deterioration had to be greatly scrapped away. The rib was placed in the damaged area.

This was a chronic infection that had developed into the usual green cancerous appearing tissue.

The May 25, 1983 biopsy was the following:

MICROSCOPIC:

Sections of specimens #2 and #3 stated to be taken from the paraspinal mass consist mainly of fibrous tissue which is heavily infiltrated by proliferating mononuclear cells, mainly lymphocytes but also plasma cells, eosinophils and histiocytes. There are also a number of Reed-Sternberg cells present; some of, which are quite typical while other, appear to be variants. There are multiple foci of fibrosis and necrosis present.

Portions of bony spicules are also present on these sections.

End of Biopsy.

I had received both the March 1983 and May 1983 biopsies from Dr. Mitri who had appeared in the medical window scene for a short time. Therefore, Dr. Mitri did not have a copy of Carl's 1977 gall bladder biopsy. Meanwhile, my husband was in intensive care, and Dr. McClarens began to explain her plan of medical action. Again the hematologist claimed that she didn't believe Carl's condition was Hodgkin's disease, and wanted to

run more tests. The Hematologist made it perfectly clear that the medical client was at the mercy of the drug prescriber when it came to the more effective antibiotic usage. The hematologist also made it clear that she would leave her patient die because of improper treatment.

I snapped my reply, "As far as I'm concerned, you lied to Carl. When he was given a choice of two hospitals, you said it didn't make any difference which one he went to. The other hospital would have begun treatment months ago, while staying with you means dying. You'll be running no more tests. We'll be changing doctors and hospitals."

What do I call a medical lie? The withholding of antitumor/antiviral antibiotics and saying that the inferior treatments were better. Hematologists and other blood specialists did check and use the checked blood for transfusions. In 1983 the Blood Type Identification was an established blood test. Shortly after and until present, it was said that they did NOT check the blood. Again, it was obvious that a second lie was used to cover-up the first lie, which, to me, could be condensed to "The destruction of the United States antibiotic policies".

Meanwhile, in 1983 when a patient was presented with distressing cancer news, the hospital had a social worker assist the patient, spouse, and family. The social worker made an introduction, and I showed her the Blood Type

Identification Card, asking, "What do each of these letters symbolize? I'm wondering if an infection is causing one of the antibodies? I realize that you may not know, but you would have an idea of who to ask."

The social worker felt that the Blood Type Identification Card was a legitimate question. She went into the pathologist's office, and then returned to me, saying, "I have just the man that you can speak with. If anyone can explain this Blood Type card, he can." The social worker showed me to his office door with the nameplate Dr. Edwards and left. I entered.

Dr. Edwards was an older gray-haired man with a foreign accent. He was sitting at his desk. The head pathologist's office was neat and attractively arranged with large bookcases. His desk sat to the right with a dark vinyl sofa at the left. Dr. Edwards motioned for me to come in and have a seat on the sofa. The pathologist placed his hand to his forehead whisking away the few dark strands among the gray that covered his temple.

He then moved his hand, pointing his fingers in my direction and saying, "There is nothing wrong with this Blood Type. I would swear on my reputation as to the creditability of everyone who works under me in the lab. I know everyone here. I was one of the first people to walk into this hospital. I came into the building before it was built." Dr. Edwards paused to look around the room, before continuing: "Matter of fact, I think I was sitting right here in this chair and the walls went up around me. Y-e-e-s-s,

I was he-r-r-e, sitting in this chair, in this very spot when the hospital was built." The pathologist changed the subject back to the Blood Type Identification. "I know all about this. I teach. I have students. There is nothing wrong here." Dr. Edwards then placed his hand on the paper on which I had written my question.

I stood up, dashing to the pathologist's side. Looking over his shoulder and pointing to the paper, I uttered, "Good, tell me about these letters DCcEe."

The pathologist reached for a book on blood typing. Quickly he opened it to a page pertaining to the Rh system, saying, "They mean nothing." It was hard for me to read a page of words in half-a-minute. My patience ran thin, as I blurted, "You said you taught. So teach! Use the big words. They won't bite." I then pointed to the letter "D" asking, "That's the Duffy system isn't it?"

"No," the pathologist shook his head, moving his finger to the Fy a+, Fy b+, and replying, "This one is the Duffy." He then moved his finger to the right and pointed to the Kidd system Jk a+, Jk b+, and continued, "I don't know what that one is." Dr. Edwards's hand moved to the left across the list of antibodies, as if the only system he could recall was the Duffy and the Rh that he had just explained.

Thus I shrugged my shoulders, saying, "I have to go. I'm supposed to be upstairs with Carl. He's leaving by ambulance."

Meanwhile, the hematologist Dr. McClarens was with Carl telling him good-bye. "Soon you'll be transferred. When you get there, they will stab you full of needles and poke holes all over your body. But, in six months, you'll be all right. Oh, by the way, your wife is crazy!"

Meanwhile on May 29, 1983, I wrote a letter to Dr. Garcia, stating that God gave me Blood Typing Identification A2DCcEe with a Warm Auto-antibody special type: +DAT with antibodies from the MNSs, Kell, Duffy, and Kidd blood groups. And I wish to know what every letter is. I also would like a copy of every test in my husband's folder. Then I went on and on, stating how good God was. And that the Lord would never hide the Truth from those who seek. Dr. Garcia was a Hindu, so I thought that the God thingy might get me copies of Carl's medical records...but it didn't!

My husband was not moved by ambulance until late afternoon June 9, 1983. On June 10, 1983, my husband and I placed two chairs in-between the two hospital-beds that were in the room. Carl wished to sit up while chatting. Carl was not happy about the move. He began telling me about the two ambulance people who carried him on the stretcher. They went to one door and the hospital personnel wouldn't let them in. They made the ambulance people go to another door for the patient's admission.

Carl had undergone a very serious back surgery, so he didn't appreciate being bounced around and left hanging in a stretcher, and left dangling lopsided on the hospital entrance stairs. Finally the hospital personnel let the ambulance people in and had Carl placed on a hospital bed. Two hematologists entered his room. Both hematologists stood with their arms folded, staring at Carl like he was Jesus Christ. They were waiting for Carl to snap his fingers, become immaculately cured, get up, and walk out the door. There was no miracle. Carl did nothing but lay there.

As Carl finished telling me about the two hematologists, one of them entered the room. It was Dr. Garcia. The hematologist walked passed us to the far end of the room. He stood by the windows, saying: "I was going to send you copies of your husband's test, but when I found out that he was coming here, I decided to wait."

"That's alright," I replied, "I'm in no rush."

Dr. Garcia looked at me and then at Carl, saying: "I take it that he takes
    this seriously!"

I was speechless that a Doctor who knew that blood transfusions were used to treat a neck tumor when antitumor/ antiviral antibiotics were available said that. Thus I blurted, "Yeah! He takes it like a patient who just received poison for medicine!"

The hematologist moved to another state. No medical records were ever sent by either the doctor or the hospital, but scads of 1983 medical bills were received. I truly believed that every hematologist knew that antitumor/antiviral antibiotics were being withheld.

I considered it strange that Betty's Invisible Medical Book described and identified Hodgkin's disease on March 1, 1979; yet, a hematologist could not identify the health problem when an infection was disintegrating bones four years later. I had always wished for a copy of my husband's 1977 gall bladder surgery report. After unsuccessfully trying to receive a copy from Dr. Walker in 1979, I had taken several steps trying elsewhere. Unfortunately, a paid-for product was not a required received product. The insurance company, like Medicare, did NOT request copies of what they were paying for!

I couldn't get an attorney to assist me with a complaint about the tainted blood transfusions that resulted from the withholding of antitumor antibiotics. The excuses ranged from "No doctor would step forward to state that antitumor/antiviral antibiotics were being withheld" to "No hematologist would identify the checked blood using special antibodies. None of the attorneys had stated that the healthcare society had removed blood test standards back in the 1970's, which was called "Let the patient beware!" My opinion was that the healthcare (medical, psychiatry, and USP) society had in 1982 included "The Bible lied when it said that 'the blood feeds the flesh'."

Instant Insanity

Chapter 6

Scurvy

When Betty flipped open her invisible medical book, the book opened to the disease "scurvy". I assumed that everybody knew that scurvy was a disease marked by inanition (exhaustion), debility (weakness), anemia (red blood cells), and edema (watery fluid in cells) of the dependent parts. The lack of vitamin C produced a spongy condition, sometimes with ulceration (an invitation to infection), of the gums and hemorrhages into the skin and from the mucous membranes. The disease was also due to a monotonous diet of salty meats.

The disease description was short. The complete page showed a human figure with the disease. Vitamin C was something that the body took in and distributed by way of the blood. Scurvy wouldn't show up in the blood as scurvy. It would show up in a Vitamin C blood test. I found it strange that neither of my medical dictionaries listed Vitamin C. So, I'll use Vitamin A as an example. The suggested range is 20-80 /100ml. The suggested range would be too great to be called personalized. I was looking for a center figure when a hematologist called it a "mean". The patient's personal number within the 20-80 ranges would be 50 in the patient's personal bible. Then when and if the blood test figure increased or decreased, it would be noticeable.

A century ago, blood was known as the vessel that carried nutrients to the flesh (tissue). All cell life feed on some kind of nutrient. There were bacteria that consumed iron, cholesterol, etc. Some bacteria will take months to grow. I found it strange that some hospitals used the electron microscope on tissue only, and not on the blood.

I had made a list of the various blood tests and established my personal figure, which would be needed because all blood tests were being lied about.

Blood test	Range	Mine
Acetone Quantitative	(0.3-2.0 mg/dL)	1.0

By the early 1950's protein chemists were in possession of the basic techniques for the determination of amino acid sequence. Acetone also was listed as Acetoacetic acid a diacetic acid found in cases of starvation or diabetes.

Blood test	Range	Mine
A/G Ratio	(1.0-2.5)	1.7
Albumin	(3.5-5.0 g/dL)	4.2

(Protein)
Aldolase   0
(Aldehyde-lyase)

Alk Phos   (14-100)   55
Alpha Amino Nitrogen (3.0-5.5)   4

Alt (SGPT)
(Serum glutamic-pyruvic transaminase)

Amylase   (25-125 mIU/mL)   75

Anion Gap   (4-14 mEq/L)   9
(A negative charge ion)

A.P.T.T.   (23.5-34.5)   29.0
(Activated partial thromboplastin time)

Ascorbic Acid   (0.4-1.5 mg/100ml)   0.9

Bromides   0
(Anion: salt of HBr)

BUN   (10-20)   15
(Blood urea nitrogen)
Scurvy   Page 3

Blood Test   Range   Mine

Calcium   (9-11 mg/dL)   10

Carbon Dioxide (24-30 mEq/liter)   27
(Content)

Carbon Dioxide (35-45 mmHg)   40
(Tenson Pco2)

Carboxyhemoglobin   (Up to 5% of total)
(When a test gives only a high figure, it's difficult to
establish a personal mean figure)

Blood Test	Range	Mine
Chloride	(96-106 mmol/L)	101
Cholesterol	(150-250 mg/100ml)	190
Cholinesterase	(0.5-1.3 pH unit)	0.8
CO2	(22.0-32.0)	25.0

(Carbon dioxide) (CO-Carbon monoxide)

CPK   (35-250)   140
(Creatine phosphokinase)

Creatine   (0.2-0.8 mg/dL)   0.5

Creatinine   (.7-1.5 mg/100 ml)   1.0
(A component of urine and the product of creatine catabolism)

Cryoglobulins   0
(Abnormal plasma proteins paraproteins characterized by precipitating gelling, or crystallizing.)

Cyanide (Serum)
Smokers   (0.006 mg/L)
(If you smoke…you don't deserve antibiotics)

Scurvy   Page 4

Blood Test	Range	Mine
DIFFERENTIAL		
Myelocytes		0/cu mm
Band Neutrophils (3.0-5.0)		4
S. Neut (Segmented Neutrophils)	(54.0-62.0)	59
Lymph (Lymphocytes)	(25.0-33.0)	30
Mono (Monocytes)	(3.0-7.0)	5

EOS (Eosinophils)	(.01-3.0)	1
Baso (Basophils)	(.0-0.5)	0.2

The Differential Series equal 100% of the total White Blood Cells. Myelocytes and Basophils are stained together, which maybe extremely hazardous to your health, if your doctor doesn't read the test properly.

Fluoride	(0.01-0.2 ug/mL)	0.1
Folate	(2.2-17.3 ng/mL)	8.0
Gentamicin	(5-8 ug/mL)	
Globulin (Protein)	(2.5-3.5)	3.0
Glucose	(70-110 mg/dL)	80
HDL (Good Cholesterol)	(30-80 mg/dL)	55
Hemoglobin (Hgb)	(13.7-17.7)	15
Blood Test	Range	Mine

Hematocrit   (40.0-52.0 %)   45.0
(Hct)

IMMUNOGLOBINS
IgG   (723.0-1685.0 dl)   1200
IgA   (60-333)   195
IgM   (45-145 dl)   95
IgD   (0.5-3.0 dl)   1.5
IgE   (0-380 ml)   150

Iron   (75-175 ug/dL)   125

Lactate (0.6-1.8)   1.1

Lactic Acid   (0.5-2.2)   1.4
(Sarcolactic)

MCV   (82-94)   88
(Mean Corpuscular Volume)

MCH   (28.0-32.0)   30
(Mean Corpuscular Hemoglobin)

MCHC   (32.8-35.2)   34
(Mean Corpuscular Hemoglobin Concentration)

pH   (7.35-7.45)   7.4

Blood Test	Range	Mine
PHOS Acid (Phosphatase, Acid)	(0-7)	3
Phosphorous	(3.0-4.5)	3.5
Platelet (PLT) (Irregularly shaped disk)	(150-350)	225
Potassium	(3.5-5.0 mEq/L)	4.2
Protein	(6.0-8.0 g/dL)	7.0
Blood Test	Range	Mine
PT (PAT) (Prothrombin Time)	(11.0-13.0)	12.0

(A glycoprotein) protein carbohydrate (conjugated proteins) Conjugated. 1) Production of two new cells; 2) Bacterial c.; 3) sexual reproduction among protozan ciliates. Typical members such as Paramecium or Balantidium Coil (a parasite of man) possess two distinctive nuclei, a macronucleus and a micronucleus.

PTT (Partial Thromboplastin Time)	(21.0-33.0)	27.0
Pyruvate	(0.3-0.9 mg/dL)	.5

RDW   (8.5-11.5)   10
(Red Blood Distribution Width)

SGOT/AST   (5-40)   31
(Serum glutamic-oxaloacetic transaminase)
(SYN Aspartate Aminotransferase)

SGPT   (7-56)   30
(Serum glutamic-pyruvic transaminase)
(SYN Alanine Aminotransperase)

Sodium   (135-145 mEq/L)   140

Sulfates   (0.8-1.2 mg/dL)   .9
(Inorganic)

Triglycerides   (40-150 mg/dL)   90
(Triacylglycerol) Tri: A prefix denoting three
Acyl: An organic radical derived from an organic acid by the
removal of the carboxylic hydroxyl group.
Glycogen: The liver normally stores about 100gm. Of
glycogen, from which glucose can be derived as needed by
the body.

TSH   (0-7 mIU/L)   3.5
(Thyroid stimulating hormone)

Blood Test   Range   Mine

UREA	(24-49)	35
UREA Nitrogen	(11-23 mg/dL)	17
URIC Acid (Uratic, Urate)	(4.5-8.0 mg/dL) Male (2.5-6.2)	6.0 Female 4.0
Vancomycin	(20-40 ug/mL)	Peak
Vitamin A	(20-80 /100 ml)	50
Vitamin B12	(180-900)	400
Zinc	(70-150)	110

It was obvious that the 1982-83 hematologist had lied about blood tests. The hematologist had used Special Checked blood for blood transfusions instead of using antitumor antibiotics to treat a neck tumor. I believed that an evil doctor was a medical terrorist that could kill more people by bad medicine (and medical lies) than anyone with bombs or bullets.

Complaints to the Health Department fell upon deaf ears and employing an attorney was impossible, so I tried the old cliché "You lie, you die. The Truth Machine will turn you into Mice Meat Pie". Remember when we were kids and were taught that lies were bad? Well maybe not everybody was taught that.

I had found the best way to detect a Medical Terrorist was to ask questions about blood tests. The evildoers would say, "Blood means nothing!"

Instant Insanity
Chapter 7
Oneself Dream

While staying at the hotel, I went to the swimming pool. As I stepped into the pool, I remembered a dream. Immediately, I visualized myself stepping into the swimming pool dream exactly as I had in a dream. The reality was as if a déjà vu. I was alone when entering the pool in both the dream and now. I interpreted the swimming-pool dream as looking-at-one-self. In reality, I didn't swim very well; therefore I walked around the five-foot-deep pool, noticing as many details as possible.

My first thought was about the sign that said, "Do not swim alone". The Grand was a big hotel. I noticed that I was the only one there, using the pool at 8 p.m. My second thought was that maybe I could drown and no one would notice. The stress disappeared as I thought about my guardian angel watching over me. My attention then wandered to my book of dreams where I actually had met the dream characters that had appeared in three different dreams. Each dream was filled with stress and each reality when they appeared was also stressful. The stress that was provoked when listening to medical lies was never properly explained; it was as if the medical lies involving the withholding of antitumor antibiotics didn't exist. I believed that medical lies were a form of corruption and Health Sabotage, and certainly involved patriotic and personal stress along with untreated pathogen produced illnesses. I didn't go to a doctor to be lied to. I expected the doctor to prescribe good medicines, not give inferior treatment that would result in continued sickness and even death!

My problem was and still is that I have no right to my most effective medicines. It was obvious that the doctors had used the prescription drug law to deprive my husband and me the right to our more effective medicines. I used my husband's medical treatment records as an example about the medical liar's information that I felt deprived me the right to my more effective medicines. It took a complete book to describe Carl's two cancers, bacterial-produced heart disease, a gall-bladder surgery, a hernia surgery, 8-inches of air accidentally in Carl's IV-line, and a biopsy that sounded as if the blood was sucked from the tissue in order to cover-up pathogen produced health problems. I certainly wished that someone had told me about the century old evil doctor's curse. Corruption worked like skin cancer. First the cell-type personal infection appeared, then the sore-type deterioration spread. After the deterioration-spread, the point-of-origin would be ignored and deliberately lied about. If the shoe was on the other foot, of course, I would be dead! So again, I prayed that every one of the medical murderers dwell with their murdered though all of eternity!

Then I remembered that I had spoken to a Mississippi nurse about my husband's 1996 Gentamicin Sulfate drug over-dosing. The nurse said that she knew that Gentamicin Sulfate only had a 10 to 12 day usage. Naturally, I told the lady (RN) that doctor's knew that Gentamicin Sulfate drug over-dosed, yet they encouraged the drug to be used on a 6-week protocol. Carl's doctors had fed the public poisoned blood test information and then poisoned medicine by encouraging prescription drug over-dosing. The nurse and I were overcome with depression, so the conversation was dropped.

Instant Insanity
Chapter 8
Writer's Workshop

To properly interpret a dream, all the details would have be remembered, properly related, and the reality information that surrounded the dreamer should be considered. I had noticed that many dream symbols identified themselves. The 1978 book dream had intrigued me, while the 1979 haunting house dream had many interesting symbols.

In 1979 I joined a writer's workshop. One member was an editor for a small magazine. When I read the "Haunting House" dream, the editor said that there was no such thing as a haunting house. My word choice was inappropriate. Therefore, the dream was immediately noticed as unusual. The dream dwelling had identified itself as "The Haunting House". At the end of the dream two men appeared, and they, too, were given an identity as "Garment Thieves".

Six years after the "Haunting House" dream, I met both men that had appeared in the dream. Prior to the meeting several things had taken place: 1) my husband had a 1977 gall bladder surgery where an infection was noticed and left untreated. 2) Carl's infection settled into a noticeable neck tumor, and later into his 1983 fourth-stage Hodgkin's disease. 3) Carl's father died in 1984. 4) The month prior to our 1985 house burglery, Carl was pulled over and arrested for drunken driving. Carl asked me to go to the State Police Barracks to get his knife so that he wouldn't be charged for a concealed weapon, too!

I had noticed that once a person was charged with drunken driving, the state police (who wear a white shirt and navy pants) had what appeared as "double bookkeeping records" in order to make the charge stick.

Carl insisted that the police would finger print his knife and he would be charged with two crimes. He claimed to be innocent of both wrong doings. So, I agreed to retrieve Carl's pocketknife, which was a little larger than normal. After I returned home with the knife, Carl then said that he was guilty!

"Guilty," I screamed! I was as irate with Carl, as I was with the Evil doctors who were withholding antitumor/antiviral antibiotics!

Carl explained that it was too expensive to argue with the lawmakers and policing agencies. He would plea guilt to the drunk driving. It was difficult to conceal it from the children. After graduating from "Drunk School", Carl was given a party and known as the daddy that wasn't a Drunk; he only got arrested for it.

The day after the November 7, 1985 meeting with the second garment thief, I received a speeding ticket and then a second speeding ticket a month or so later.

Instant Insanity

Chapter 9

The Haunting House

The Haunting House

For three consecutive nights, the same dream appeared. It was about a house that I had purchased without ever seeing the outside of the building. The intriguing thing about the 1979 dream was the discovery of the ever-changing stairways to the attic, even though the basement stairs always remained the same.

In the dream, I had moved into an old haunted house that the dream called "The Haunting House". The scene was as if I was watching myself on TV. I could see myself entering the living room and standing there amazed and shocked that the dusty, dilapidated, and degrading dwelling was my new home. Then I could hear myself say: "Remember what you liked about the house when you first saw it."

I looked around and saw dusty white sheets covering the furniture. An old fireplace decorated the far wall. I walked to the fireplace and ran my right hand down the grimy dark-plaster wall. "No," I answered. "I don't remember ever seeing anything like this. Now, you tell me that I've bought it!"

I was too awestruck to remove the dusty white sheets to look at the furniture. I shook my head in distress as I investigated the fireplace of my newly purchased home. Again I moved my hand along the wall next to the fireplace. I touched a button to a doorway that triggered some kind of secret wall-panel open. The entrance led to a secret passage. A foyer sat in the hidden half of the first floor level. There were two wooden stairways. One led downward to the basement, while the other went up to the attic. I stepped in the direction of the attic. Halfway up the stairs, I noticed something that I thought was an ordinary window. It was new for an old house. As I looked at the new and shiny glass, the dream identified the window as a 'mirror-glass'. I looked closer at the 'mirror-glass' that identified itself as the 'shattering image.'

The way the window had presented itself, I thought that the window itself had spoken, so I lingered to examine the 'mirror-glass'. I looked it all over and saw absolutely nothing unusual. To me, it was a new window that was added to an old house. I looked outside. The trimmed lawn was decorated with four large old oak trees.

"Pretty scenery," I said and continued up the stairs. I found myself in the attic. I looked around at the old wooden walls that connected to the ceiling, showing the plywood roof that formed the roof's slant. Old items were stacked and stored along the walls. Many of the items were unfamiliar to me. There were old-framed pictures of nobody I knew, although I did recognize a very old sewing machine and very old wooden rocking horse. The center of the attic contained only a large black chest with no other items near it. I opened the chest. It was filled with old Renaissance-style gowns that were made of velvet with satin or lace trim. I held up the first garment. It was stunning. Then I picked up the next gown, thinking how out-of-place these old items were compared to the other old stored items. I picked up and examined one garment after another until I reached the bottom item and it fell apart into rags. Immediately, I thought, "Well, if one clothing item fell apart, they're all probably going to fall apart."

So I folded the things and placed them back into the black chest. There was nothing else of interest in the attic, and I returned down the staircase passing the 'mirror-glass' again. The 'mirror-glass' itself was like a puzzle. I looked out the window and the scenery had changed. The four oak trees had lifted their limbs. I could see more trimmed grass, and the lawn had widened. I noticed it; yet, because it seemed unimportant, I proceeded down the stairs to the basement.

The unfamiliar basement was a spooky place. A special closed door led into a small hidden room within the basement walls. Chills ran down my spine, as I turned the doorknob. I entered the small secret room by pushing the cobwebs aside. The room was absolutely filled with cobwebs. Fortunately, there were no spiders or any other crawly creatures.

Cautiously I surveyed the room's contents. Something about the room's aura was absolutely hideous; yet, I couldn't see exactly what it was. My heart beat rapidly, as fear weakened by body. My brain spun with wild images of terror. I wanted to leave. Not just leave the room, but go from the house! I still could not believe that I had purchased this hideous house. Then all of a sudden something in the room drew me in like a magnet. I stepped completely inside. The air was filled with meaning and hidden words were saying, "This is your new home. If you leave now and don't look back, you will never see that the time you spent here will be the happiest time of your life."

I calmed down and thoroughly examined the basement's treasure room. Along with cobwebs covering every corner, dust covered a long three-foot high dresser. The one and only furniture item ran the complete length of the wall. On top of the dresser sat an old wooden jewelry box. I opened the sturdy, well-made container. Inside the items were dazing bracelets, necklaces, and rings made of gold, silver, and diamonds. The treasure room also had a small closet. I opened the door. There was enough light in the closet for me to quickly see that it was empty. I closed the closet door, noticing that there were no light fixtures. Yes, I noticed the light in the empty closet and the light inside the small basement room; still, that seemed unimportant.

On the third night the haunting-house dream appeared, I was again in the basement and looking for the light source when I heard: "The foyer." My searching was interrupted as I was again drawn me to the foyer upstairs. The foyer contained nothing. So I wandered up a few steps higher to the 'mirror-glass." The scenery had again changed. This time

I could see that the green fields and rolling hills had been turned into dirt. Nothing hindered the vision. The trees were no longer in the scenery. Still, I thought nothing of the scenic change, until the 'mirror-glass' spoke: "Look through the glass into the shattering image on the other side."

I was already upset with the idea that I had purchased this house without ever seeing the inside or outside. The words disturbed me, and I answered the 'mirror-glass', "I have to go out today. I know that I mustn't leave the house unguarded, but I must go."

I pushed all thoughts aside and left the dwelling. When I returned, it was the first time that I viewed the outside of my newly purchased home. It was totally run-down and in shambles. Meanwhile, the dream's aura informed me that my house had been broken into while I was away. The window next to the main entrance was smashed. Why the intruders broke the window to enter the house baffled me. The caulking around the window was old, cracked, and hanging down the glass pane. The window could have been easily pried loose. The black shutters were loose and hanging tilted in front of the curtain where the burglars had entered.

I rushed inside. Upon my entering the house, I saw the hidden door next to the fireplace wide open. There were three stairways to the attic: "no steps," "the spiral stone steps," and the standard wooden steps." The secret hallway leading to the attic had been discovered and the burglars had used the standard wooden steps. I dashed through the open door and up the secret hallway. I stopped halfway up the stairs by the 'mirror-glass' and looked out the window.

Again the trees had moved their limbs, and a paved street was below the window. Parked next to the curb was a light-blue car. The two thieves who had broken into The Haunting House were just now leaving. One thief was opening the right-hand car door. I could see that he was a large-framed man dressed in a white shirt and dark-blue pants. The second thief wore a light-brown suit. He was closing the car trunk with all the antique garments inside. The second man then walked to the left-hand door (the driver's seat), watching for traffic while doing so. As he opened the driver's door, the intruder turned his head and I saw half his face. The two male thieves proceeded to drive away.

I continued up the stairs to the attic. The black chest was open. All the good antique garments were gone. Also taken were some old pictures and the unidentifiable miscellaneous relics. I could see myself picking up the scrap cloth material that was strewn about the room. The dream's breath whispered, "All that's left are the rags."

Immediately, I remembered the box of treasures in the basement secret room. I dashed downstairs. The basement door was fully opened. The secret room had been discovered, yet none of its treasures were touched. I could see my dreamself walking inside. I was puzzled and wondering how the treasures could have been seen and then overlooked?

Then I noticed that a red illuminating gas that seeped through the wooden panels produced the dim light. I stood examining the light's reflection. Nothing at all had been touched. Not a cobweb was disturbed. I could not understand how a treasure such as this was discovered, then overlooked! End of 1979 dream

- -

I liked the dream because of all the symbolisms. It had appeared two months after the detailed-diagram book dream. The dream used several unclear words, one of which was Haunting "ever continuing", and another was "dream's breathe", which I interpreted to be when the dream itself spoke. I had kept the dream in the basement next to my typewriter, which was in a room separate from the main part of the walkout basement. My vocabulary was limited and unclear. An example would be the word "burglarized" meaning unlawfully entered.

Six years after the dream (1985), our neighborhood had a neighborhood watch and it was fortunate for my husband and me that several neighbors were watching my house when a blue car drove into my driveway and a black passenger entered my house. The neighbors knew that no one was home; so after they called the police, one called me to let me know that my house was almost burglarized. She said that even though the intruder who had entered the house had completely disappeared, the police had everything under control, but I probably should come home anyway.

I hung up the phone saying: "My house is being burglarized, and have to go home."

I arrived home to a driveway filled with police cars. So I parked across the street at my neighbor's. She was standing outside. The neighbors filled me in on all the details. The intruder had entered the house. Apparently, he walked into the master bedroom and saw my white jewelry box on the dresser. As he opened the box and was handling the jewelry, he looked out the window and noticed a police car pulling into the driveway. The intruder threw the jewelry back into the box and raced into the family room and ran outside through the back glass doorway. Outside the door wall was a half-empty enclosed wooden wood-box. There was enough room for the six-foot intruder to climb in and hide, which he did.

As the neighbors were filling me in on their details, I noticed that one car parked in my driveway was a burgundy Pontiac. Later, I was under the impression that the burgundy Pontiac belonged to the investigating officer. But when I saw the burgundy Pontiac, I immediately thought of a friend who had the same kind of a vehicle.

My husband and I had a friend who owned the exact same kind and color car. I was standing about 200 feet from the blue car, and trees were blocking my view. So I quickly walked down my driveway to make sure that it wasn't our friends, and to get a clearer understanding of what was taking place.

A man in a gray suit (I assumed that he was a police detective) was holding a handgun on three men standing by the blue car that my neighbors had described as the intruder's car. I discovered that all four figures were totally unknown to me, as I blurted, "I don't know you!"

The investigator holding the gun became a little nervous, while looking at me as if to ask, "How are you?"

Then one of the intruders said, "Our friend is dating the girl that lives here."

"What?" I screeched, "Our daughter just turned 12 today. She doesn't date anybody. Who the hell are you?"

Inside my house, someone standing by the picture window waved his arm, and the officer holding the gun said, "You can go in now."

I entered my house by way of the kitchen. The first person I saw was dressed in a deputy's uniform. The man was standing by the fireplace holding a shotgun. The second man I saw was dressed in a light-brown suit. My thoughts quickly flashed to the man that I had seen as the garment thief in the dream that I had titled "The Haunting House". I then stumbled over my dog Spot, a white and black colored Pekingese. I picked up my little dog so that I wouldn't step on him again. I was shocked, it was as if I had just walked into a dream, and I was dumbfounded.

The investigating officer, Sergeant Thomas-- the garment thief, asked if anything appeared missing. As Sergeant spoke, he was flipping his fingers while his partner took notes. I remembered that the garment thief had a partner who was dressed in a white shirt with navy trousers. I didn't recognize both garment thieves. I had already met his partner the month before. I then thought of valuables and remembered that all the treasures were in the basement. The basement stairs were off the kitchen. I turned and dashed down the basement steps. The dream's presence was all around me. I could feel the Dream State, but I couldn't figure out what it was saying, especially with the garment thief being the investigating officer. The small room where the valuables were kept had not been entered. The dream titled "The Haunting House" sat by the typewriter untouched. Nothing at all was disturbed in the basement. The only thing disturbed was by the outside doorway. The once opened drapes were now shut. I returned upstairs still carrying my little dog like Dorothy in "The Wizard of Oz."

The investigating officer motioned for me to enter the bedroom. Apparently, the first thing a burglar would do would look for the master bedroom, hoping to find money and jewelry. I had two jewelry boxes. A large white one sat on the long dresser and a large gold colored one in the closet. Sergeant H opened the closet door, asking again if anything was taken. He pointed to the second gold-color jewelry box that I kept on the upper shelf and the attic at the same time. The dream's breath reappeared, and a voice called down from the attic, "All that is left are the rags."

My real life attic has "no stairs." I was then totally dumbfounded and speechless. So when the investigating officer asked if I was staying home. All I could do was nod my head to answer "yes."

Then the investigating officer thought about two neighbors stating that they saw someone enter the house, so he called in a dog. When the canine arrived, the dog sniffed and found "the woodbox visitor" (the disappeared intruder) three feet outside the back door. The four intruders left in a police car. All four were laughing and waving to my neighbors and me as they drove off.

The next day I called the investigator. I was informed that all four suspects were released. The man hiding inside the woodbox had said that he was never inside the house, and that the detectives would be wasting their time fingerprinting. There were two clear handprints on the glass door-wall, which may have been done by the woodbox visitor.

"What," I questioned, "the burglar tells you how to investigate?"

The detective snapped a second reply: "He must have been wearing gloves."

One poorly spoken word led to another, at first it was said that there was no law about someone visiting a wood box. When "the woodbox visitor" went to court, my neighbors and I received a summons to appear. I wasn't asked any questions. Only one neighbor went into the courtroom. She was surprised that the only questions the judge asked her were about ME. Yep, by the time I finished explaining it, the judge couldn't tell who the burglar was 1) the woodbox visitor, 2) the investigating officer, or 3) me!

The Sheriff's Department officers placed charges against "the woodbox visitor" and he was sentenced to six months.

Then when I went to court to pay my speeding tickets, I mouthed off about the law enforcer supporting a drug law that removed a personal right to the more effective medicines. Then I paid my traffic fines and scratched it up to a "Streak of Bad Luck."

The 1985 burglary and 2 motor vehicle violation tickets were within 2 months and they were 2 years after I complained to the Department of Licensing and Regulations about the 1983 very noticeable withholding of antitumor antibiotics.

I was disappointed with those designated to uphold the law. I looked up the Ten Commandments, and whispered them to myself.

1) Thou shall have no other Gods before ME, the Lord.
2) Thou shall not make unto thee any graven image.
3) Thou shall not misuse or abuse God's name.
4) Remember the Sabbath day, to keep it holy.
5) Thou shall honor thy father and thy mother.
6) Thou shall not kill.
7) Thou shall not commit adultery.
8) Thou shall not steal.
9) Thou shall not bear false witness.
10) Thou shall not covet.

What I had found interesting about the philosophy of the Catholic religion, they stated that they did NOT teach the tenth commandment. They mixed the ninth and tenth commandment, because a church was a covenant. A building has expenses and has to collect money.

The US drug law created a medical god that could be easily identified as a doctor/drug prescriber. The doctors philosophy would be you do NOT see what you do NOT look at or for. They must have took the word NOT from each of the commandments and added them to medicines and medical advice. Beginning with the NOT wishing that a tuberculosis vaccine would be discovered, and then NOT wanting one used when one was. Then they added the word "NOT" to the use of effective antibiotics.

Apparel: Dreams of apparel denote that enterprises will be successes or failures, as the apparel seems to be whole and clean, or soiled and threadbare. If you reject out-of-date apparel, you will outgrow present environments and enter into new relations, new enterprises and new loves, which will transform you into a different person.

Cobwebs: Foretells deceitful friends will work you loss and displeasure.

Diamonds: To dream of owning diamonds is a very propitious dream, signifying great honor and recognition from high places. To lose diamonds, and not find them again, is an unlucky dream.

Emerald: To dream of an emerald, you will inherit property concerning which there will be some trouble with others.

God: To dream that God sends his spirit upon you, great changes in your beliefs will take place. If God speaks to you, beware that you do not fall into condemnation. Business of all sorts will take an unfavorable turn. It is the forerunner of the weakening of health and may mean early dissolution.

Gold: If you handle gold in your dream, you will be usually successful in all enterprises.

Green: Is a hopeful sign of prosperity and happiness.

House: Usually is oneself. An old and dilapidated house, denote failure in business or any effort, and declining health. [A family – family tradition] [Ancestry – domestic establishment]

Loss: To dream of the loss of any article of apparel, denotes disturbances in your business and love affairs.

Natural: Be careful to note whether the objects are looking natural. The newly added window was out-of-place for a very old house.

Ruby: To dream of a ruby, foretells you will be lucky in speculations of business or love.

Silver: Is a warning against depending too largely on money for real happiness and/or contentment.

Stairs: Up means good fortune. Down is unlucky.

Thief: To dream of being a thief and that you are pursued by officers, is a sign that you will meet reverses in business, and your social relations will be unpleasant.

White: Denotes sadness.

Instant Insanity

Chapter 10

Definition of a Friend

Because of the two medical lies that had taken place in 1977 and Carl's 1982-1983 neck tumor treatment that had manifested into a cancerous condition, I felt that evil doctors had used the prescription drug law to withhold antitumor antibiotics and create medical lies. Prior to Carl's second cancer, I was writing five reasons why I felt that a hematologist could incorporate Health Sabotage with false information. 1) The hematologist used the United States prescription drug law to withhold antitumor/antiviral antibiotics. 2) The hematologist lied about what the pathogens that had appeared in the blood meant. 3) The hematologist checked the blood to use special antibodies. The special antibodies also had a meaning. When a medical person stated that the blood wasn't check, they were lying. The changing of reality to a lie, I called a lie. 4) The laboratories raised blood test tolerance figures to camouflage disease-produced pathogens. 5) The hematologist could discard needed medical records.

All accessible medical records were considered Medical History.

As I wrote each item, the withholding of gram-negative antibiotics that were incorporated reminded me of the cover, which were two pictures with a plastic overlay in order to view both subject. Without the plastic overlay, both subjects would not be properly viewed. In reality, the five listed items were not properly viewed when Carl was the patient. If Carl were deprived of antitumor antibiotics, then I would be too. What would the ultimate goal of a medical liar be? All I could think of was Health Sabotage. The goal of Health Sabotage would be the destruction of the United States antibiotic/vaccine policies. Indeed, a United States enemy's delight, all the enemy would have to do would be to become the official drug dictator and then substitute good medicines with poisoned. The medical liars such as Dr. Rodriguez and Dr. McClarens were already there.

Who would notice?

In July 1994, my husband again appeared sick. After having cancer once, he was fearful that the cancer had returned. Carl was undergoing several medical tests, when my younger brother, Elijah, called. Younger brother was a 37-year-old into-himself-type person. Elijah was a RN by profession and he was also into the short-class of bodybuilding. Younger brother, who was 15 years younger than Carl, knew about Carl's first cancer and that in 1983 the hematologist had used blood transfusions with "Special Antibodies" to treat Carl's neck tumor until there was enough infection to disintegrate bones!

Carl condensed their conversation: "Oh, you think you might have cancer. Well, if you divorce my sister. I would understand. We all know how squirrelly she gets." Carl then changed the subject, by saying, "You are from the most coldest, most heartless family that I have ever met!"

It sounded to me that if a person worked in the medical society, the job required that the person lie about the withholding of antitumor/antiviral antibiotics, all blood tests (including the ones used prior to transfusions), and any person who questioned the medical lies were called crazy. Carl also had a sister who was a nurse.

In 1994 and prior to Carl's second cancer, his son was in Somalia. While Duane was in Somalia, his mother-in-law Kate was diagnosed with breast cancer. I had shown Kate's daughter Carl's 1983 Blood-Type-Identification card. The card was a symbol that there was an established blood test in 1983. I was under the impression that all blood had antibodies; some people had more antibodies than other. Antibodies were known to produce immunities. On two occasions I had tried to have my blood checked for antibodies, and the replies were that I didn't have any and that the Blood Type Identification was done on special occasions.

Kate and her daughter visited Carl's sister for breast cancer information. Apparently Carl's sister had told Kate that Carl didn't have fourth-stage Hodgkin's disease. When Kate saw Carl she asked him. Carl then had to explain that when the doctor's told Carl that he was fourth-stage, he was not aware that the staging was from 1 to 4 and he thought that the staging was from 1 to 10. So, Carl had replied, "That's not too bad!"

Strange as it sounded, Carl's sister also told Kate (a breast cancer patient) that the hematologist Dr. McClarens never checked the blood used for her brother's

blood transfusions. It shocked me that a nurse would look at a Blood-Type-Identification card, and state the known special antibodies were not there. It was like someone stating that you don't see what you are looking at. It was like a person saying that infections were non-existent. So if you have breast cancer, don't worry about it. Simply listen to your cancer doctor, and go out and find happiness whether. Immediately, I thought that the medical lies were a great plot for a story idea titled "Suicide Made in the USA".

Meanwhile, I became baffled with the word "Friend". Does a friend leave a friend or a family member to die?

The answer was obviously, "Yes."

I became totally fascinated with the word "friendship". First I looked the word up in the dictionary: A person whom one knows well and is found of; love; close acquaintance. In reality, people judge a friend by what they do, not what they say (of course, a friend does not lie to you). I couldn't understand why any family member would tell Carl that the hematologist didn't check the blood. The blood was checked several times, including the transfused units.

Then I looked for as many "friend" references as I could find. I was told that the word "Dumb Frenchman" came out of the Second World War, which younger brother's words appeared to be. Mother was French and Father had always referred to the words "Dumb Frenchman" because of the Second World War.

So, I read about the French and the Second World War. The French were famous for their Bohemian Tarot and their Catholic Spiritual Insight; yet, when the Germans marching into France, saying, "I am your friend." In five days, it was a COUP D ETAT. The word "friend" was transformed to "You are now my slave!"

World War II was an era when more people died to disease and famine, and the word "Friend" showed how a lie could push a country's people into a quick enemy victory. Since the Second World War, the definition of a Friend has never been the same. I lived in the USA where effective antibiotics were being deliberately withheld, and the medical people were deliberately lying about it. To hear a "Yes" answer to the question "Does a friend leave a family member die to a medical liar" bothered me.

I thought that maybe God would tell me the true definition of a friend. HE, the Deity-God would live in the Heavens someplace. The Lord's covenant would be as large as the universe and as vast as eternity. God's love I had heard was ever lasting. In scripture, when a human-built-covenant conflicted with the Lord, God would send a messenger to tell about the misery and the stress that the pack (the ungodly) had made upon the people.

The messenger would tell about the wrong doing and ending the prophecy with "The Lord said to remove your covenant."

I felt that leaving a friend die to a liar who withheld the more effective antibiotics was a wrongdoing.

As I dreamt, I prayed for the simple truth. It was a clear sunny, great day for traveling. With the "friendship" problem in hand, I journeyed to the Heavens to get my answer from the Big Man. I was like the scarecrow in the Wizard of Oz, walking on a cloud-covered path going before the Lord in the land of the Big Icons.

I knew I was on the right path; when I looked down to see the clouds beneath my feet. I glanced to my right and then my left to see the mountains and the hills, too, were white cloud formations. In the distance, I could hear the heavenly drummers. The sound was similar to my rapid heartbeat. As I approached closer, the drummer's music became a thunderous roaring sound like a loud angry foot stomping tune. I could see the hillsides sloping downward to each side of the path upon which I walked. On top of each hill was a familiar manner-styled, winged angel clothed in a long, white gown. They looked similar although I knew not why. Everything looked familiar. Suddenly, each angel flipped its wings to flutter from the hilltop. One flew down from the left and the other coasted to my right. I could tell by the song words that they knew why I was here. The Angels didn't talk, they softly sung: "Here comes a thief. Here comes a thief."

I joined the angels in their song, swaying to the now softened drummer's beat. Immediately, I thought, maybe they didn't notice the garments I wore. I was dressed much differently with a cream-colored T-shirt and navy slacks. As the three of us approached God's city, I heard the angels change their words.

Quickly I thought that they were trying to trick me and stop my journey to the Lord. I, too, changed my words, singing along: "I am a thief. I am a thief, going before the Lord."

The drummer's music stopped, and there I was facing the Lord. His eyes were clear and magnetizing. I had never seen Eyes like that before. For a moment, I stared. I could see though His eyes into a dimension that was vast beyond anything my little brain could comprehend. The sky with its wondrous clouds could be viewed in the background. Then I looked back upon His face.

There He stood in His magnificence. The Lord had two Arms, until He lifted them. Then they became huge and his Hands were like shelves. To His right were the endless items of passion and glory. On His left were the stored and endless stacked items that were less often used. Again, my little brain couldn't hold a fraction of what I saw.

The two Angels moved forward and encircled above His Head, casting an aura as if to say, "Here is God." Soft music filled the air, as the two Angels continued to circle, singing sweet and low, "Jesus died for you. Now, you will die for Thee."

All I wanted to know was the definition of a friend. Does a friend leave a family member to die to the liars? It saddened me to think that I, as an American was one who didn't know the true meaning of a friend, so I said: "All I want to know is the definition of a friend."

I saw a White Horse standing at the Lord's left, which would be facing my right. The angels glided to the horse, again gathering in a circle of song: "Ride, ride the white horse, singing, Praise, Praise the Lord."

There was a small shadowy-creature that was sneaking into the scene. The creature was an out-of-place thing. The dream then identified the creature as being something from the other side of Heaven. The creature hid behind a small white rock formation. The out-of-place creature kept moving the rock until it was in back of the White Horse. I could faintly hear the small, shadowy figure humming in a low whispering tune: "You've got the best part."

My attention returned to the purpose of my visit. All I wanted to know was the meaning of a friend. I wasn't expecting finely tuned details. "I don't know what to do," I said to the Lord. "I'm lost, and I don't know the meaning of a 'friend'. I'm lost and need advice. What is a poor scarecrow to do?"

"Ride the White Horse, singing like the angels do. Don't you remember? We did this once before. All you have to do is say, 'Praise the Lord.' That's it. I will send the angels with you to tutor you along. You should NOT get confused. There is nothing complicated here. If you don't hear the angels sing, and you are lost for words, you can always hum the FOREVER song."

"Huh-h," I questioned, "The Forever Song?"

Yes. It's a one-word song 'FOREVER'. So tell me now, if you cannot do it. I will then send the other rider. Mount the White Horse and go. Oh, one important thing: if you get off the White Horse for any reason, it'll be your Doom! You don't play a thief twice with me."

That was my friend down there. The Medical Monopoly Society with their lying ways would be killing my friend. So I had the angels place me on the awaiting, already saddled white mount, and I rode from the Heavens to Earth with my song: "Ride, ride the white horse, singing Praise, Praise the Lord."
End of dream.

I woke from the dream, thinking that it was as upsetting as the reality. So, I tried to interpret the dream.

Dream Interpretation:
God: To me, God represents truth.

White: The color white represents truth, protection, guidance, and the Light of God. I was writing about the people wearing white called doctors, and not telling the truth.

Horse: To mount a horse bareback, you will gain wealth and ease by hard struggles.

Little out-of-place creature: The dream gave the creature's identification as "the creature from the other side of Heaven".

Best Friend: In this case the best friend was Self. It was obvious that if the shoe were on the other foot, every family member would leave me die to the Medical Liar's Society. For me to leave my husband die, then the same lies would soon be upon myself.

Then I remembered there was music. "What kind of musical tune did I hear?"

It was a raging heartbeat sound. Once I discovered that medical history was being lied about, it upset me! I was awestruck to discover that the prescription drug law was used to deprive my husband and me the right to our more effective medicines!

The United States antibiotic policies had all the symptoms of being under an enemy's control. In 1983, a hematologist was my worst nightmare in living reality. Then I thought about three subjects: God (truth), My Right to Effective

Antibiotics, and Medical Liars. I remembered Charleston Heston in the movie "The Ten Commandments". I had to look them up. 1) 2) 3) 4) 5) 6) 7) 8) 9) 10)

My conclusion was simple. The Lawmaker made a doctor/drug prescriber the official United States god when they passed the United States prescription drug law. The drug prescriber covenant had their own 10 Commandments, which was similar to the Ten

Commandments; only the word NOT was removed. The United States prescription drug law gave the prescription god the right to lie and to comment murder, as such was Carl's 1983 case. If Carl remained under the hematologist who used blood transfusions to treat a neck tumor, he would have been dead.

Then I thought again about "Does a friend leave a family member to die?". The answer here was again "yes".

I had dug out an old dream titled "Class Reunion", which again forewarned Carl's death. If Carl didn't go to the doctor, he would die. I showed the dream to our daughter. She and I tried to get Carl to go to a doctor/drug prescriber. We all know that life was terminal. Antibiotics weren't an answer to everything; yet, when a doctor lied about them, I wondered why the lie! To die because the United States had lost the Cold War to Health Saboteurs would indeed be a horse of a different color.

Meanwhile, Carl was building a deck on the front of the house to occupy his mind from a fearful hospital dilemma.

Finally the decision was made that Carl had a malignant tumor, and that he should go into the hospital to have the tumor removed. At the time of Carl's second cancer, the hospital laboratory had raised a blood test figure 10 times what the figure should have been. Therefore, the tumor-produced cancer condition was not cancerous enough to be treated with any antitumor/antiviral antibiotics.

Again blood tests were lied about and again Carl left the hospital without any antibiotics.

Instant Insanity

Chapter 11

God Visits

At the time of this 1994 dream, Carl had had his second cancer surgery and was still in the hospital. His cancer was again caused by a tumor that had turned the tissue malignant. Again no antitumor antibiotics were prescribed.

The World Trade Center was first bombed in 1993. President Clinton knew that the American Heart was known as "Organ Thieves" throughout the world. The United States people needed organs to replace the bacterial-damaged organs. At this same time, infant vaccines contained Too Many Germs and were leaving infants blind and deft. Reality was that it was known that all cells mutated, yet, it was said that antibiotics were ineffective.

An example of an over-used antibiotic would be Gentimicin Sulfate USP. Gentimicin was known as a short-term (2-3 week) antibiotic. The US medical advisors placed the short-term antibiotic on a 6-week protocol. (In my husband's 1996 commonly known bacterial-produced heart disease case, he was drug over-dosed.) In the 1960's, it was known that cells mutated and that new antibiotics could be made from the new cell germs. Yet, the drug-of-choice was one that was known to create additional problems.

In 1994, the cost to run a computer search about antibiotic history at a Medical Library was $65-per-hour. I thought that the money-figure was extremely pricey… the same search only cost $25-per-hour at a Connecticut Medical Library. I felt that government medical information should have been less expensive and more available. The antitumor/antiviral antibiotic called Adriamycin was found as Doxorubicin in the TOXNET N.L.M.'s toxicology Date Network under the Hazardous Substances Data Bank.

The man who had hung the 1974 sign on the mutated/sibling antitumor antibiotic named Adriamycin/Doxorubicin must have been the president or CEO of the organization: "Copyright 1974-year, MICROMEDEX, Inc.". I would like to know what he looks like, after meeting two of the three faces in the dream. Now onto the dream titled "God Visits".

As I slept, I could visualize my dreamself walking up a brightly lit hospital corridor. I was following behind like a television cameraperson who was recording the movie shot. My dreamself was dressed in a black turtleneck with matching black slacks, and a black bandanna covering my hair. My dreamself was dressed as a thief, going to a Pirate's Carnival Fest. I followed, hoping that my dreamself would lead me to the disappeared Adriamycin. All of a sudden my dreamself stopped halfway up the hospital hall, as the dream informed that the party was through the left wall and one floor up. My dreamself then turned to the left and proceeded to walk through the left wall.

Again I followed. Poof…The scene changed to darkness. Soon I, too, was on the other side and one-floor-up at the pirate's party fest. The complete left wall was covered with white medicine cabinets, making musical sounds. I was standing in back of the room watching and listening to the pirate's music fest. The room was filled with firm-foot-stomping rhythm of power and wealth to a pirate's song. It was an interesting tune of folly and play. There was a melodious whisper behind each white door that sounded like a humming chorus, "I am your god". Meanwhile, each cupboard door pompously warbled its own chorale verse: "A thief has his wealth, plus the wealth that he stole." The second cupboard door joined with its verse: "A liar's song is designed to tear truth into shreds." Each door added an unrecognized verse, such as, "Be He male, he'd be Satan from hell, be it the other…the angel of Death," but the song's ending was very clear: "Make me your murder and I will kill you all."

The last sentence scared me, as I realized that they were real, live pirates. I looked around. I had lost my dreamself at the Pirate's Fest. Quickly, I started looking for an exit by turning to the right.

The white doors on the left wall disappeared, as I turned to face a large archway. I was wondering where I was, when the dream called the place: "the chemotherapy cabinet."

The room identified the white cabinets as: A medical covenant built by a group of people who have made a pact to withhold medicines in order to build a medical job security bank by closing the door to common-sense drug usage in relationship to humanistic healthcare values. A place where medical customers were not allowed to enter or to know truthful medicine history.

I stood facing a large dark archway. There was no "exit" sign. Large 3-foot feathers, symbolizing a heavenly-gift/ prize/treasure, hung across the top and halfway down each side.

The feathers represented themselves as medical gifts. The feathers also identified that they didn't belong to the person who had hung them. Each father was once a heavenly gift that fell to earth as a prize, a gift, and a golden treasure. The thief's gift was presented as a plague. Since each feather was identified as a separate item, I looked each feather over for an understandable meaning. The feather's original meaning and content had been rearranged. It appeared as garble. Only the person upon whom the prize was bestowed knew the original feather meaning. The feathers couldn't speak; yet, it was as if the feathers themselves were stating that the original owner or meaning was nowhere around, and that they were deliberately placed out of reach with their original medical design hidden.

I stepped back to take a quick count. There were between twenty and twenty-five feathers, and each one had been neatly nailed in place around the archway.

Again, I watched myself examining each feather over and over while saying, "One feather is Adriamycin." I even began to examine the feathers wondering if I was looking for a pill.

The feather at the archway center was the most eye-catching. It had far more layers of dust and cobwebs than any of the others. The reds and yellows showed the discoloration of considerable age. The shades of blues and greens remained slightly lustrous. The center feather itself gave me the impression that it had been hanging in the Humanity-in-Reverse-Cupboard for an extremely long time.

Again, I stepped back from the feathers. There was a problem with the cupboard's language. Then the dream again called the uninterpretable garbled words: "Humanity-in-Reverse-Cupboard."

The only thing I could clearly see was dust, feather size, and feather luster. The newly added last feather on the left side of the archway had an eye-catching rainbow metallic hue. I stared at all the feathers, saying, "No, I'm not leaving until I find it. It's here! I know it is. To come this far and not thoroughly examine each item would be foolishness."

I began looking again and carefully examining each feather. I could feel by the aura that the one item for which I was searching was there among the many feathers. I was totally baffled as to why I could not recognize it.

Then all of a sudden, the dream began to speak in a narrative voice: "First, I want you to meet the person who hung the feather for which you look."

A distinguished-looking man dressed in a gray business suit walked into the center of the dream through the feathered dark archway. He was carrying a 2'x1' white sign, with the numbers "1974."

The feathers had been moved and strung across the cupboard-room like a banner. The dark-haired man walked from the center to the right and stepped to a feather that was hanging three or four feathers to the right of the center. There he hung his 1974 sign. The unique business-looking gentleman then turned to face me, as the dream introduced his name and continued to narrate: "When you steal from God, do not think it goes unnoticed."

A second man came walking in. He, too, was carrying a 2'x1' white sign. I didn't see any lettering. The sign appeared blank.

A third person, a shorter, dark-haired woman followed quickly behind. She, too, carried a 2'x1' white sign with no visual print. I saw the right side of her soft, sweet facial features and her mid-length dark, flowing hair as she walked pass, and continued to walk to a second archway on the extreme right that lead back into the bright hospital corridor.

The second and third person had entered the dream quickly and were exiting when a fourth figure entered the dream holding a 2'x1' sign reading "1994." The faceless figure entered moving to the left, and stood in the shadows. It represented the newest hung feather.

I could feel myself thinking aloud and wondering, "Who are these people?"

I turned my head back to the right to see that the second man and the woman did not stop to claim a feather, they exited the dream through the bright archway that lead back into the hospital corridor. The narrator said each name and told of a special place where these people were kept, saying, "They will be called upon when the truth is searched."

I did not see the place to which the two walked. Once they passed through the hospital corridor archway, both disappeared. My attention then focused at the left and on the 1994 sign. I was in awe at the fourth profile standing by the most recent and brightly rainbow-colored bottom feather. It was as if that bright feather itself cast metallic hues, deliberately letting me know that it was the newest addition: "The best of the penicillin for the largest of the blood groups is now Humanity-in-Reverse."

I stared at the silhouette. It was like a self-image of me; the last of the blood groups was my own.

The narrator continued: "The humanity cupboard is now empty. The book is in its entirety and ready to be written backwards. Stealing from God is like stealing from your neighbor. The thieves should be handled like any other thief. The crime should appear in print. The items they stole and who they stole them from."

A nine-foot god-like figure moved, re-appearing, under the feathered banner that was strung from the dark archway to the brightly lit one. The figure was the dream's narrator, saying: "What is my World War, 2, doing here?"

The word "2" had an echo: II, two, to, and too. When the narrator spoke, it was more than a pun. The words spanned from earth to eternity.

The dream itself cast an aura, as if it, too, could speak, identifying the narrator: "When this figure walks, the ground will tremble."

The scene became like a large computer room, lighting up each circuit until the final function flashed "Glow" and the complete room lit every corner of the "how" and "why" the chemotherapy covenant had come into existence and that the covenant itself was the "Doom's Day Message."

The dream spanned to beyond my recognition. The only thing understandable was condensed to one sentence: "after death there will be no readers".

End of Dream

At the time of the 1994 dream, the hospital laboratory in had raised a differential white blood cell called the Basophil tolerance level figure 10X's the amount of what the figure should have been.

So, I wrote all over the world to see what figures other countries were using. Strange as it may sound, the lowest figure with the reference of "Steven ML. Fundamentals of Clinical Hematology" showing the basophils were 0-0.5. Meanwhile, the highest figure came from a hematologist in the United Kingdom (UK) with the reference of 0-0.8.

In 1995, the dream's dark-haired woman who carried the white 2'x1' sign appeared. She was the emergency room doctor. Her name was Gayleand she was Carl's doctor at the time of his 911 emergency hospital visit. Again, the white blood cell tolerance level figure was 10x what it should have been; therefore the increased patient's abnormal cell count went unnoticed.

I was then under the impression that every patient's blood test that was done would have abnormal cell count go unnoticed because of the extremely high lab figure used. I complained to the health advisors.

My husband's 1995 blood test was as follows:

Test	Patients	Realist Figures	Increased Figures
Neutrophils	68.5*	57-67	30-80
Lymphocytes	20.2	25-33	20-60
Monocytes	8.2	3-7	2-10
Eosinophils	1.5	1-3	.01-5.00
Basophils	1.7*	0-0.5	.01-5.00

*The 1.7% was not flagged as abnormal because the high tolerance level figure was again raised to 5% instead of 0.5, which I figured as ½%.

In 1996, the man in the dream who was carrying the blank sign appeared. He was an Internal Medicine doctor at the hospital. When the Internal Medicine doctor drew my husband's blood, the differential blood test system used was similar to the one that the UK hematologist had sent:

Test	Patient	UK	Lab's
Neutrophils	9.2H	2.4-6.2	2.0-9.0
Lymphocytes	0.5	1.1-3.3	0.4-3.5
Monocytes	0.5	0.14-0.7	0.0-1.0
Eosinophils	0.0*	0.02-0.3	0.0-0.5
Basophils	0.0*	0-0.08	0.0-0.2

*The cell activity that had appeared on my husband's 1994

and 1995 blood tests had completely disappeared. The year 1996 was a year after I had complained to the Department of Licensing and Regulations about the laboratories raising blood test figures.

In 1996 and the month prior to meeting the man who carried the blank 2'x1' sign, Carl had dreamt that he died. Meanwhile, the drug-of-choice Gentimicin Sulfate USP was known to drug over-dose after 2-3 weeks of use. Yet, it was placed on a 6-week protocol to treat endocarditis. Drugs are federal. If the drug-of-choice was used from 1993 to 2001 and drug over-dosed the endocarditis patients, it should have been noticed in the other 49 states, too. The common-bacterial-produced heart disease called Endocarditis had a low survival rate.

I would call a medical liar a "Health Saboteur", whereas a religious person might call the Health Saboteur "The Anti-Christ", using the reference Leviticus 17.11 "For the life of the flesh is in the blood". I believe that the Anti-Christ would say the opposite "Blood means nothing", meaning that all three Anti-Christ, Health Saboteur, or Medical Liar would make a logical reason about how "Blood means nothing", and the most important thing would be the destruction of the United States antibiotic and vaccine policies.

The World Trade Center was bombed in 1993 and again in 2001. Yet, the drug-of-choice Gentimicin Sulfate USP that was to be used, as a short-term drug remained unnoticed that it was used on a longer-term protocol that would drug over-dose the patient halfway through the 6-week recommended treatment. I would compare a medical liar with a terrorist.

The 1983 hematologist's actions reflected that the United States prescription drug law was used for more than to withhold effective antibiotics/medicines. One drug prescriber specialist would lie and another doctor would swear that the lie was the truth.

I continued to interpret this dream. To me, God represents "priorities and truth". There were two 1994 dreams where God appeared. In my titled dream "Definition of a Friend", God's eyes were open with a clear and with a wide vision beyond my comprehension. In "God Visits", the dream's narrator's eyes were dark and with no vision, yet, the room lit-up showing where all the lies were stored.

My first thought to the dark eyes was blindness. When the United States (US) lawmakers passed the US prescription drug law, they were depriving the people of gram-negative antibiotics.

Then I tried to identify the feathers, which was when I found the 1908 BCG Vaccine: a vaccine introduced in France about 1908 by Bacillus Calmette-Guerin. The Calmette-Guerin bacillus used is a live attenuated strain of the Mycobacterium tuberculosis. It may be given to infants who are especially exposed to the risk of tuberculous infection and to young people who are shown by the tuberculin test to have no natural immunity to the disease. It may be given to all medical students, veterinary students and nurses who have no natural immunity and come into contact with tuberculosis. It is not used in the United States because chemical means of prevention are considered more effective and do not interfere with the skin test used in epidemiology and private practice as a single means to test incidence of infection in the population.

New diseases would be created with normal cell mutations and chemicals. Blood tests would be the patient's personal bible. A medical evildoer would say: "Blood does not feed the flesh. Blood means nothing!"

Instant Insanity

Chapter 12

Tijuana (1995)

A year after Carl's second tumor-produced cancer and a year prior to his common bacterial-produced heart disease, it was obvious that antitumor antibiotics were being withheld. I wanted to purchase antibiotics in Mexico.

It was also known that a hospital laboratory had raised a white blood cell figure 10 times the normal figure; and a medical person had told Carl that when your doctor doesn't prescribe antibiotics, it's because you don't need any antibiotics. Yet, the medical people never mentioned the antitumor/antiviral antibiotics discovered in the 1960's.

My husband's 1995 blood tests was the following:

TEST RESULTS LAB INCREASE
(Lab Normal) PERSONALIZED

Neutrophils	68.5	30-80	(54-62)	59
Lymphocytes	20.2	20-60	(25-33)	30

Monocytes	8.2	2-10	(3-7)	5
Eosinophils	1.5	.01-5.00	(.01-3)	1
Basophils	1.7*	.01-5.00**	(0-0.5)	0.2***

* Patients was not flagged because of the lab's increased figures.
** 10 times higher than 0.5.
*** Again, Carl had left the hospital without antibiotics.

I wrote all over the world to see what other places were using. The highest figure came from a UK hematologist who stated 0-0.8. Strange as it may sound, the lowest figure came with the reference of "Steven ML. Fundamentals of
Clinical Hematology" showing the basophils were 0-0.5.

I, too, had a tooth infection in 1988, and cell abnormalities were also showing up in my blood tests. A blood test would be like a person's personal health bible. A person needed to know what a normal cell range would be, before identifying cell abnormalities.

Both my husband and I had a White Blood Cell normal range of about 6. Therefore when the White Blood Cell count raised to 8, it was personally high, especially when the infections were long-termed and untreated. I had made it clear that I wished to go to Mexico to purchase what I considered to be the more effective antibiotics, which were Adriamycin, Penicillin Benzathine, and Streptomycin.

My husband Carl and I had spent two months in Laughlin, Nevada, which was about 2200 miles from Michigan. Then Carl and I headed for Tijuana by driving from Laughlin to Florida.

We were cruising down US5 when we saw a big green sign with white bold print stating: last exit before border. We drove down the ramp onto a side street and into a Motel 6 parking lot about three-and-a-half blocks from the Mexican border. Carl and I rented a room for two nights. We were tired after the 360-mile ride from Laughlin.

The next day, Carl asked the motel clerk the best way to go to Tijuana. The clerk suggested that we leave the vehicle in the motel parking lot and take a cab to the border. While Carl was asking, I was outside walking around and looking at the scenery.

I couldn't see the border and there was a walkway over the highway US5. So, I walked halfway across the walkway and stood over the middle of the highway, looking for the Mexico border. I'd never been to Mexico and it was obvious that I was

going to have to get closer to see it.

The cab arrived. Carl and I got in, and he drove three blocks to a large fairly vacant parking lot to let us out. "Where do we go from here?" I asked.

The cab driver pointed to a distant building, saying, "Go to the money exchange."

The building was far away. There was a bus with a Tijuana sign and a man standing next to the door, a few steps from where Carl and I stood. I rushed over to the stranger and asked him where the money exchange place was.

The bus driver told Carl and me that unless we were going to buy a big-ticket item, there was no need to exchange currency. He then suggested that for two dollars a person we could purchase a round trip ticket to the center of Tijuana. The buses ran every half hour to Tijuana and back to the United States until nine o'clock at night. Since Carl and I had left the car at the motel, instead of going to the money exchange, we boarded the bus.

I was impressed how quickly we drove through customs with no questions asked and I was hoping that the return trip would be as easy. I have been over the Canadian border and usually someone says something to you. I looked down at my knitted slacks and small purse, thinking that I couldn't carry much dressed like this and on foot. I had heard that antibiotics were cheap in Mexico, so I decided that I wouldn't be spending over $100, in case purchases were questioned.

The bus began making turns down several city streets. I didn't think about writing any of the names down. Soon there were too many for me to remember. The bus stopped and the driver announced that a bus would be leaving for the U.S. every half hour. All we had to do was return to the bus stop on Revolutionary Street and that the last bus back was at nine o'clock.

Carl and I toured Tijuana. The street was lined with shops and a peddler stood in front of every store, saying, "Come inside and see my establishment."

Carl and I would shake our heads, replying, "No."

One shop had a Mexican band by the entrance. I wanted to listen to the Spanish music, so Carl and I walked in. As we entered, the musicians stopped. Carl and I walked around the various stores inside. A black leather cowboy hat caught my eye. I picked it up to look at the $28 price tag. The merchant asked, "You want to buy the hat?"

"No. It's too much."

The merchant then looked at Carl, asking if he wanted to buy his girl friend a present. Carl told him "No", and that I was his wife.

The retailer then asked: "Then how about something for your neighbors wife?" Again, Carl only shook his head.

The merchant quickly began pushing his wares, "This is a real good hat. It's genuine leather." He pulled out his lighter, and began torching the hat. "See. See. The flame didn't hurt the leather."

"You keep trying to burn it and I know I'm not going to want to buy that one. It's too expensive anyway." I exclaimed and proceeded to walk away.

"How much did you want to pay?"

I wanted to buy something for my daughter, but I didn't know if she would like the cowboy hat style. "Five dollars," I replied.

We bickered for a while. I ended up paying $12, and walked around Tijuana with a black leather hat.

Carl and I walked upstairs to a bar/restaurant. They had a special where you purchased one margaRita and received a second free.

We sat on the open porch overlooking the busy street. I heard a whistle blowing. A mobile bartender sold tequila shots from the bottle directly into a patron's mouth, blowing a whistle until the purchaser said "enough." Then the bartender would shake the drinker's head.

One problem about drinking: what goes in must come out. The bathroom stalls had no toilet paper. The toilet paper was on a wall outside the stalls. In this bathroom, the attendant handed it to you. The next bathroom had no attendant. So, if you didn't know to take the toilet paper with you before entering the stall, then you were simply without!

Carl and I finished our drinks and left.

Carl stood on the sidewalk, while I walked into the first drugstore. I was looking for three antibiotics Adriamycin,

Penicillin G Benzathine, and Streptomycin. They used to be available in the United States. Can you imagine going to a U.S. doctor that would prescribe four penicillin benzathine pills, that would be take one pill a week for 4 weeks. I was under the impression that the taking of one penicillin pill a week was a good reason for its disappearance. As for the other two antibiotics, consumption would be a little more complicated.

The first druggist tried to sell me a tube of Penicillin ointment. I was annoyed that a gram-positive antibiotic was offered instead of a gram-negative one. So I left purchasing nothing. By the time that I walked into the third drugstore, Carl was doing a pacing, disgusting number, and saying, "When a doctor tells you that you don't need antibiotics... you don't need any! Only a stupid person would think they do, when they don't"

So, I quickly went inside and purchased two antibiotics that I wasn't looking for, but they were made in the USA. I purchased them because of the Mexican's suggestion: "They're better than nothing!"

Carl and I walked passed only two doors and there was another bar. Carl wanted to do something that he wanted to do. I looked at my watch. It was only three. We had plenty of time for a beer or two before catching the nine o'clock bus in seven hours.

The front of the building was completely open. Carl and I walked around the U-shaped bar to the back, which faced the street. We sat observing the establishment and passing tourist. There was a slender Mexican with a neatly trimmed mustache who sat at the corner about four feet from Carl. He looked about thirty and wore a purple shirt trimmed with a tan collar and cuffs. I noticed that he wasn't paying for any drinks. Thus I mentioned to Carl that he must have something to do with the owning or managing of the bar. Beer was a dollar a bottle, so Carl purchased three Corona's, one for each of us; and the bartender offered the three of us a shot of tequila. I turned down the shot and looked at my watch. It was 3:15. We still had time for another beer before catching the bus.

Carl began talking to his newfound Spanish speaking friend. For 8-hours Carl's conservation consisted of four subjects: I was loco. Carl had not had so much fun since his dog died. Martin asked how long Carl and I had been married. The reply was "Twenty-seven years." We had been married for as long as Martin was old. Carl constantly asked that I take a picture of his Mexican friend Martin. The photos came out showing various stages of drunkenness.

When Carl told Martin that he had not had so much fun since his dog died for the third time, Martin looked puzzled. He did not speak good English and he could not understand what Carl was saying. So I reached into my purse and pulled out my Spanish translator. With calculator in hand, I walked to Martin and entered word by word:

I have not had so much fun since my dog died!

With another puzzled look, Martin replied, "Dog die; that's sad."

But the subject was changed when Martin was impressed with the pocket electronic Spanish-English translator.

"It goes from Spanish to English, too," I said, pointing to the calculator and trying to encourage Martin to spell something so we could understand what he was saying. A language barrier overwhelmed our conversation. Thus I ended my brief chat.

Then a Mexican guitarist came into the bar. He asked Carl if he wanted a song sung to his love.

Carl raised his right hand, pointing up one finger, inquiring the price, "One dollar."

"Si."

"OK," Carl agreed and handed him a dollar.

The guitarist began naming several Spanish songs. He wanted us to choose one. All the titles were totally unfamiliar. So, we insisted that he pick the one he liked.

Martin, Carl and I had a few more Coronas. Again I passed on the tequila shots. I looked at my watch. It was 6 o'clock. I noticed several people had entered. Each wore a white shirt and the words "SECURITY" written across the back. "Look at those shirts," I said, pointing them out to Carl. "They have as many employees as there are customers. We have bars in Michigan that will hire extra security during the busy hours. Look at all the security and it's only six o'clock."

Carl nodded, commenting: "It must be a busy bar." Shortly, the bar was filled with people.

I decided to run across the street to a liquor store to purchase two quarts of Tequila while Carl remained talking to his newfound Mexican buddy. After I returned, Carl excused himself to go to the men's bathroom. I waited and waited until one of the male employees told me that my husband was on the other side of the bar. I walked around the bar. And standing next to Carl was a young slender senoRita clothed in a red dress. The dark-haired girl looked at me with a facial expression of "O-o-o-p-s." Then she slipped away to blend in with the large crowd.

Carl was purchasing two red margaRitas. I asked him, "Why are you buying two margaRitas when you have a beer at the other side of the bar?"

I picked up both margaRitas and we returned to our original bar stools. As I was just finishing the second margaRita, a bar employee tapped me on the arm to let me know that it was 11:00p.m.

We missed the bus. Oh, my God. I panicked. Grabbing Carl's arm to get his attention, I said that we had to leave. By this time, Martin had his head on the bar passed out. Martin was not moving; he lived there, we didn't! Finally, Carl was able to get up. Thus Carl and I struggled through the crowd to the street. On the sidewalk was a large dumpster. Carl put both arms up and clutched the dumpster, holding onto the sides and saying, "I can't walk!"

"Well, try to remember how real quick," I snapped. "It's one foot, then the other for three miles to the U.S. border."

Carl took a few steps sideways, then a few steps backwards. Fortunately a taxi cab driver came up to us, asking, "Do you want a cab?"

"Yes," I nodded. We walked to his cab and got in. He drove us to the US5 section of the 8-lane border highway were he had to turn around and we had to get out in the middle of the highway where there was a row of market shops.

A young Mexican boy about twelve came over, asking, "Do you need some help?"

I examined the faded red sweatshirt with the yellow lettering "United States" and replied, "Yes. Your shirt says where I'm going. How do I get there?"

The young lad offered to get on one side of Carl, so that we could help him walk straight. The boy kept saying: "I can only go so far."

The lad spoke very good English. He pointed to where the custom building was, and then ran off. I stood looking at four lanes of bumper-to-bumper traffic. There was an overpass, but I couldn't see any stairs. The young boy returned with a young friend. The four of us weave through the four lanes of traffic. Again the young lad said: "We can only go so far."

"How far is only so far?" I asked.

"This far. We have to leave you now. The law says that we cannot enter the U.S. custom building.

A young couple was about 75 feet in front of us. They were walking in the direction of the customs building.

"See that couple, Carl? See how nice they are walking? That is what we have to do."

The young couple entered the building. We were still about 75 feet behind. Once Carl and I were in the building, I took Carl's hand to encourage him to walk faster, hopefully straighter.

Instead Carl began shaking my hand to make me let go, saying: "You're going to make me fall down."

By that time we were in back of the young couple at the custom-US-entrance crossing. There were two American guards at the crossing, one on each side railing. The male guard facing us, said: "These people don't have anything to claim."

Carl and I had quickly passed through the custom crossing, and walked outside. We then crossed the street. Carl stopped to balance himself on a large blue mailbox and told me that he had to pee.

I no sooner said, "So. So pee!"
When I could hear voices in back of me, whispering: "Is he going to pee?"
I turned to see where the several voices were coming from. There were at least six people sitting at the walk's edge. Carl and I noticed that there was a Jack-In-The-Box across the street that we had just crossed. So we walked back and into the eatery. Once inside, I saw the men's room and several chairs facing the restrooms. I walked to a chair and sat down. Carl slowly walked along the wall, fumbling to find the room.

Carl looked at me asking "Where?"

"Try where the sign says 'Men'," I said. At that moment two men exited. I pointed, saying, "Where those two men just walked out of."

Carl proceeded to enter the restroom as a security guard approached me, stating: "You know, in Mexico they arrest people for drunkenness."

"Thank you for that information," I said, nodding.

I didn't think about asking the security guard about U.S. cabs. The cabs were available in Tijuana, and I didn't see any cabs after we had crossed the border. So, when Carl rejoined me, we ate hamburgs and left. Once outside, Carl and I walked down a sidewalk that turned into a dirt walkway along railroad tracks. "Don't stagger," I told him, "we don't want to look drunk. Look around. You and I are in a dark section of a border town by the railroad tracks----lost! You know, some people might be slightly fearful of being mugged."

Since, I grew up in the inner city of Springfield, Massachusetts. This was a good time to try my Italian cousins philosophy. Walk like you're a member of the Mafia, and if that don't work then you run like the wind.

There were no direction signs. I thought that we were walking the wrong way. So, I walked ahead of Carl to save him a few steps. Sure enough, we were going the wrong way. When I returned to tell him that we'd try the other street, Carl had fallen down and was complaining about breaking his eyeglasses and cutting his face. Carl's German blood was beginning to show as he said, "Give me a cigarette."

"I don't have any."

Carl continued to complain, "You left me. This is all your fault."

"Leaving you, would have been back in Tijuana holding onto the dumpster at midnight." I snapped, pointing to a gas station and saying, "Maybe they sell cigarettes over there."

The gas station looked open. We walked up to the small building's bulletproof-glassed cashier window. "Do you sell cigarettes?" I asked, while looking around for a cigarette machine.

The short, blonde man behind the glass petition was extremely nervous and his body and head shook, "No."

"You don't!" I blurted, shocked.

Quickly he responded, "You have to go down to the next gas station."

Turning to Carl, I added, "I don't believe this. Lost. No cigarettes, and he's more scared than we are!"

We continued our walk. When two people are bickering, they fail to notice the tail-tale logical signs. As we continued down the street, I heard the highway traffic that I had been so desperately listening for earlier. "Stop," I said and stood surveying the scenery.

Carl, too, could hear the vehicle sounds too. Looking behind us, I could see the overpass walkway, which I had stood on earlier. We backtracked and became unlost when we found US5. We crossed the highway on the walkway, and found our truck with the cigarettes inside.

Instant Insanity
Chapter 13
I dreamt I died

Decades of medical lies could produce nightmares. In order for the dreamer, such as myself, to evaluate the accuracy of the nightmare, I would have to have the medical records in front of me. After an Maine County hematologist that used the 1950's prescription drug law to withhold antitumor/antiviral antibiotics in order to discover a new disease treated my husband, I had discovered that the blood tests were the easiest for me to read.

I also read that the discovery of DNA tests were known to be extremely accurate, while blood tests weren't. One reason could be because laboratory figures had a lengthy range of tolerance level figures that was called normal. According to the Bible "Life of the flesh is in the blood".

Blood tests would be similar to a personal health bible. We lived in a high-tech world were DNA tests were discovered after blood tests were. Therefore, a person would need all their blood test reports in order to determine a personal bible blood-test figure.

The normal White Blood Cell figures for my husband and I would be about six, whereas the blood-test-laboratory would be stating a 10-or-11 for someone else. By the time my husband or my blood test reached 10, there would be an infection in the blood. Dreams could assist with identifying the health problem severity. The magnitude of the sickness would show up in reality on his or her medical records, especially when comparing the old and new blood test figures. The comparing of old and new blood test revealed the patient/medical customer's increased figures as well as the blood test laboratory specialist's inconsistencies.

A dreamer could go back into a dream to ask questions in order to receive new areas or to review old areas to research after waking. Death dreams would be consider serious dreams, and should be investigated thoroughly.

Carl had a dream in April 1996 that I titled "I dreamt I died".

Poor Carl. His dream must have been filled with pain and gore. Carl lifted his right arm and waved his hand signifying that the death was too horrifying to repeat. "Finally I died and was placed peacefully inside a cushioned coffin buried beneath the earth," Carl said. "I wasn't there very long, maybe a couple months, when I heard shoveling. Someone was digging up the ground to my coffin. The coffin door was opened by a nurse, saying, 'Sorry to disturb you. But your wife said that we didn't do a test, so we're going to do it now.'

"I was pulled from my grave, the test was done, and I was re-buried. Two months later, I was dug up again. It was the nurse again, saying, 'your wife says that we didn't do this test right. Now we have to disturb you for a test re-do.' Again I was re-buried, and again two month later dug up. 'Sorry to disturb you again. But your wife says that this test disappeared, now we have to do the test again.' All I know is that I feel real sick now!"

For eons, dreams have forwarded the sick and the dying that Death approached. I decided to change my attention from blood tests to focus on Carl's dream by looking up the dream symbol meanings:

Being the Victim: Feeling victimized.

Body: Our body represents physical life; the process which causes growth and aging.

Buried: Letting go of the past or repressing painful experience within.

Coffin: A reminder of one's own mortality.

Dead Body: Our skin or shape is felt as our boundary, the edge of our universe.

Death: The death of some aspect of our outer or inner life.

Digging up Ritual: Similar to initiation. It reveals the deeper levels of oneself. A digging-up ceremony that required reality digs to our attention.

Shovel: The digging into our memories to uncover our past experience.

Sleep: Foretells sickness and broken engagements.

Underground: You are in danger of losing reputation and fortune.

Uniform: Denotes that you will have influential friends to aid you in obtaining your desires.

Stranger: Unknown aspect of oneself.

Time (two month): The passage of time in our life.

Since I was familiar with the importance of blood tests, I wished for more areas to research about the increased laboratory figures. In 1995, I had again complained to the Department of Licensing and Regulations. The 1995 complaint was about the Maine County hospital laboratory raising a blood test figure 10 times what the figure should have been. The 1995 complaint appeared to fall upon deaf ears. Unless, it was something that the Health Department had already know about for the last few decades. The lawmakers passed more unpatriotic medical laws.

Meanwhile, I believed that medical liars would fall under the category of Health Saboteurs and the Bible version of the Anti-Christ. I could have and probably swore the medical anti-Christ up-and-down, but it didn't help. Legalized Health Sabotage was legalized Health Sabotage!

Medical history revealed that doctors have been lying to their patients and the public since the discovery of the 1908 tuberculosis vaccine. When a medical person said that the

BCG vaccine was occasionally used and the fact was that it was never used, that medical person would be called a liar!

As I was searching for a better explanation to the 10 times laboratory cell figure increase, I, too, had a death dream appeared. I titled both Carl and my dream: "I Dreamt I Died".

In my death dream, I was speaking to my husband and two of our friends; when I woke I couldn't remember who the two friends were. Anyway, in the dream, I sat upon a backless wooden stool, while my husband and the two friends were standing. The four of us were looking out a large glass window and viewing a mile of meadow.

I remembered telling the three of them that I could run that mile, come back, and explain the basophil-blood-subject better. You know how dreams are; it was a blur. Yet, I ran the mile, came back short-winded, and continued the conversation with the other three.

In the midst of the conversation, I had a massive heart attack. I fell backwards off the stool, telling the three: "You have to get my differential blood test now. The basophil blood activity will continue in relationship with the pathogenic microorganism invasion. This cell activity will continue only for a short time: after that, a proper reading will be forever lost. I want to know how long 'after death' it will take before my blood basophils reaches the laboratory recommended 5.0 tolerance figure."

In the dream, the other three people were awestruck that I was dead, and so was I. My eyes were in total shock to see my dreamself dead. Immediately, I stated to tell my dreamself to get up. I didn't. So I waved my hand in an upward motion while saying, "Get up. Get up!"

The dream informed that when you are dead, you do not get up.

End of Dream.

What I had found interesting about my dream was that any hospital anyplace in the world could check to see how long it would take a sick or dead person's blood to reach the 5% basophil figure.

At the time of my husband's dream, his medical problem was Endocarditis. The bacterial-damage-hole-in-his-heart was difficult to diagnose. Medical history was also that at the 1993 World Trade Center bombing, the drug-of-choice to treat Endocarditis was Gentamicin Sulfate USP. It was known to be a short-term (10-to-12-day antibiotic). The Gentamicin Sulfate USP was known to drug over-dose halfway through the recommended (6-week) treatment protocol.

Instant Insanity
Chapter 14
May 15, 1996

A "then and now" dream appeared about coordinating and comparing the chapter titled May 15, 1996 with fiction and reality. As soon as the dream used the word "Coordinating", I knew the blood test subject was complicated. Sometimes dreams inspired me to investigate the authenticity of reality. The dream I titled "God Visits" contained more accuracy than the words that medical specialist spoke. Dreams aroused the differences between what was real and what was merely fantasy. The United States Congress passed the prescription drug law CAUTION: Federal law prohibits dispensing without prescription, during the Korean War. The question then as now "What effect did the prescription drug law have on United States antibiotic, patriotic, and vaccine policies?"

First, I coordinated the blood test reality, then I tried to remember what might appear as fiction. My first guess was the day after Carl cadaver body part replacement surgery, which would have been July 10, 1996. Death had taken a human figure form as a man wearing a black cowboy hat. Death and a dying man (who wore a brown cowboy hat) had entered Carl's hospital room. The words that Death had told the dying man were smeared as written words on the wall. The written words were a vision. There was also a vision in 1998 when a spacey dagger appeared. First, the blood test reality:

May 15, 1996 was when I met the second person that was a man carrying the blank 2'X1' white sign that appeared in the "God Visits" dream. He was a doctor at the hospital. My husband's blood test was the following:

TEST	RESULT	RANGE	(BRITISH)	(MEAN)
White Blood Cells	10.2			
Neutrophils	9.2 H	2.0-9.0	(2.4-6.2)	3.0
Lymphocytes	0.5	0.4-3.5	(1.1-3.3)	2.1
Monocytes	0.5	0.0-1.0	(0.14-0.7)	0.36
Eosinophils	0.0	0.0-0.5	(0.02-0.3)	0.14
Basophils	0.0	0.0-0.2	(0-0.08)	0.03

The white blood cell activity called the Eosinophils and Basophils had disappeared, and an infection that had encircled and was destroying Carl's heart was going unnoticed.

The British hematologist's information was greatly appreciated. The foreign hematologist had found the establishing of a personal blood test figure interesting. There were different blood test methods used.

The prior year (1995) I had met the dark haired woman carrying the blank 2'X1' white sign that appeared in the "God Visits" dream. She was the emergency room doctor at the hospital. At the 1995 time, blood tests were again done and again a laboratory figure was raised 10 times the normal figure and again blood abnormalities were not flagged. Again, Carl left the hospital without antibiotics.

My husband's blood test was the following:

TEST	RESULTS	LAB INCREASE	(Lab Normal)	PERSONAL BIBLE
Neutrophils	68.5	30-80	(54-62)	59
Lymphocytes	20.2	20-60	(25-33)	30
Monocytes	8.2	2-10	(3-7)	5
Eosinophils	1.5	.01-5.00	(.01-3)	1
Basophils	1.7	.01-5.00	(0-0.5)	0.2*

*Notice the White Cell Basophils personalized figure when compared with his more accurate personal-bible figure, when compared with the Laboratory high figure of 5%.

At the time (1994) of the "God Visits" dream, my husband's blood test was the following:

TEST	RESULT	LAB INCREASE	Lab Normal	PERSONAL BIBLE
White Blood Cells	8.4	4.5-11.0	(4.5-10.0)	6
Platelet Count	285	140-400	(150-350)	225
Neutrophils	68.7	30-80	(54-62)	59
Lymphocytes	16.3	20-60	(25-33)	30
Monocytes	12.9	2-20	(3-7)	5

| Eosinophils | 1.1 | .01-5.00 | (.01-3) | 1 |
| Basophils | .9 | .01-5.00 | (0-0.5)* | 0.2** |

*Basophils high tolerance level. A 5% was used on the blood test instead of the suggested normal high of 0.5%.
**Notice the decimal point

In less than two months after meeting the second man on May 15, 1996, my husband needed a cadaver body part to replace the bacterial damage done. The 1974 subject of withholding antitumor/antiviral antibiotics had manifested to surgically removing bacterial-infections. The permitting of bacteria to destroy organs had become popular and profitable.

After I had met the 1995 doctor dream person in reality, I began writing all over the world to see what white-blood-cell differential figures other countries used. In April 1996 my husband had a death dream. Also in April, I had received a letter from a British hematologist. He compared both country figures and referred to the figure that I was looking for as mine as a mean. What should a person do with medical lies that were used to cover-up the purpose of a blood test?

Miley, our college child, was in her room. I knocked and put her light on as I entered. Miley was lying in bed and watching television. "I have a problem and I would like your opinion, "I said, waving the British hematologist's two-page letter. In my eyes, medical lies that remained lies were a Death Wish that my generation was leaving to hers.

I handed daughter the British hematologist informative letter and sat Indian style on the floor, waiting for her reply, which was: "Mother, it's because you don't listen."

"You didn't turn to the second page," I snapped, "Will you please read the letter first? Then throw in your opinion!"

After daughter read what I thought was only the first paragraph, she gave another opinion: "Mother you not only don't know how to listen, but you have problems reading, and you leave out the fact that people have feelings. Like the other day, you made me feel like dad's sickness is my entire fault."

Immediately, I remembered the snowstorm and daughter's added aggravation. So I refreshed both our memories by saying, "To go out in a heavy snow storm when you don't have to go any place, and have dad and I push on your truck so that you can get out of the driveway was annoying. Your dad was sick and was thinking that he was dying, and knowing your dad he probably is! Now back to the British hematologist's letter. Your dad's blood-bacterial level was over the high level for over two years and remained untreated. My problem: I don't know if I should tell him or what I should do with this tid-bit of information."

Again daughter replied: "It's because you don't listen. Now, I listened to you, and I even read the complete letter."

So, I again pointed to the 1994 and 1995 blood tests that showed cell activity. The Hospital's 1996 blood test had showed that same cell activity as disappeared!

Miley shook her head, answering, "Now that's exactly what I mean. You did not listen. We both know that the doctors will not come here. We know that the only place that we can go is to the doctor/drug prescriber. If the doctor wishes to prescribe poison, then we all will simply have to die!"

I stood up and proceeded to leave when daughter reminded: "Now shut off my light on your way out. Remember, you turned it on when you entered."

My thoughts rambled about the Mutated Theory. I had paid as much as $169 for a drug prescriber to write penicillin (Gram-positive) prescription. After receiving the written prescription, I was then able to go to a drug store and pay an additional $10 for the penicillin. The one penicillin prescription was not enough antibiotics. I felt that a second prescription for the Gram-negative bacterial activity should have also been written, but I had no access to any except the one that the doctor prescribed. The Mutated Theory about the American brain that used 20% penicillin and 0% human brain was annoying. It was similar to a cold war side effect. The medical specialists were inserting chaos and mistruth into blood tests and medicine. People were forced to abide and die to a drug prescriber dictatorship.

It was simply an extension of the century-old evil doctor's curse: "I'll see you and your siblings sick and dead before I see you receive the 1908 tuberculosis vaccine."

Meanwhile, Carl was receiving more false information. A Larry from a well-known medical association in Chicago had called. I was not home, and my husband answered the phone. Between my husband Carl and Larry from Chicago, they decided that all penicillin history came from Dana Pil, who was Polish. Dana Pil was most noted for her work in radioactivity about 1903, which was when she won the Nobel Prize in Physics. The country she lived in was France.

When my husband told me about his conversation with Larry, I went to the bookcase for an encyclopedia and returned, saying, "Under the Nobel prize winners for Physiology or medicine dated 1945, you will find the names Sir Alexander Fleming, Ernst Chain, and Sir Howard Florey. You do not see the name Dana Pil! After listening to you guys, I'll stick with my 'God Visits' dream and the areas that God tells me to research!"

A few years later (1998), I ran into Cousin Matthew who had found the dream titled "God Visits" interesting. The words began to twist, turning to mockery about the Dream's accuracy when it was compared with Medical History Reality. Shortly, crazy backstabbing Cousin Matthew from Alberta accused me of knifing him in the back. Of course, I felt that it was he who knifed me.

Well, you know how dreams go. In a finger-snap, a spacey dagger appeared in my right hand. A spacey dagger could be thrown through space from Michigan to Alberta. The dagger itself represented that when thrown "it" would hit the heart. The thought about throwing the spacey dagger's straight shot to the heart appeared. I was that angry with Cousin Matthew's backstabbing accusation and in reality I was surrounded with medical liars.

As I pulled my arm back to throw the dagger, Cousin Matthew had putted Cousin Robert in front of him. So I didn't throw the dagger, but wondered why the vision?

Instant Insanity

Chapter 15

Miami Clinic

June 11, 1996

I began having needle-like pains shooting through my chest-heart-area muscles. Then my twenty-two-year-old daughter, Miley, gave comforting words as she nervously fluffed her long blonde hair and asked, "Mother, I'm stressed over Dad's sickness, and I need to talk with someone; will you go with me to the Miami Clinic?"

I remembered that in 1983, it was suggested that cancer patients and their family members should receive counseling, since cancer can affect children, too. There was never a doubt that it had an effect on mine. Miley was young in 1983; she was only age nine. I was under the impression that cancer questions improperly answered could tear families apart. I was under the impression that unanswered questions created many additional family problems. In Carl's 1983 fourth-stage Hodgkin's disease case, our questions were never properly answered. I felt that the hematologist and pathologist had

lied about the Blood Type Identification Card that was used to identify antibodies prior to Carl's blood transfusions. Both the hematologist and pathologist knew that antitumor antibiotics were available when the blood transfusions with special antibodies were used as a treatment mode.

"Yes," I replied to Miley's question about the Miami Clinic.

Miley's face lit up, as she said, "Good, because I've made an appointment for both of us. Gee, I can't believe that you're willing to go with me this easily."

Her remark surprised me. Miley's dad's two previous cancers had a big effect on the complete family. Now Carl was sick with a common-bacterial-produced heart disease called Endocarditis. The untreated bacteria had attacked Carl's heart. So, I looked up the Miami Clinic in the telephone book, which listed the clinic's complete name as the Miami Psychiatric Clinic. Since meeting with the hematologist, Doctor McClarens, I believed that some very reputable medical healthcare specialists were lying.

I believed that a medical evil group had existed for at least 90 years. They dated back to 1908 when the medical search was for a tuberculosis vaccine. To me, this Anti-Christ was continuing what I considered could now be a 90-year-old Medicine-For-Profit tradition. The medical evildoers also deprived me of my right to my most effective medicines.

In 1908 the doctors never wished for a tuberculosis vaccine when tuberculosis was the #1 or the #2 disease killer. The Bible gave several references to God, Blood and Lies. I would call the bloody liars who date back to 1900, "Health Saboteurs", but it would make more sense to call the Health Saboteurs "medical terrorists". The medical evildoers needed a United States president and his Congress to pass the prescription drug law to legalize medical lies in the other 49 states. An example of legal drug over-dosing would be the Gentamicin Sulfate USP short-term (10-12 days) antibiotic that was placed on a 6-week protocol to treat a bacterial-produced disease. At that point in time (June 11, 1996) Carl was in the process of being Gentamicin drug over-dosed.

I gathered the medical information on Miley's dad. Carl's Blood Type Identification, his last three blood tests, and I included a Haitian voodoo doll with four voodoo pins.

Miley and I drove in separate vehicles to the Miami Psychiatric Clinic, a fairly new looking red brick building next to the hospital.

When we entered, Miley spoke with the receptionist about our appointment. The receptionist checked her appointment list and gave Miley a lengthy form. Miley and I walked to two empty chairs in the waiting room. We sat down and began looking over the lengthy form. First I asked, "Why only one name and one form?"

"Duh-h-h, your insurance company is paying for the visit, and they told me

that both personal visits would be combined under one name."

"That's a very good point," I said, as I stood up and walked to the receptionist.

The receptionist checked my insurance card and said, "Yes. The $126-per-hour service charge was covered."

I returned to the chair next to Miley, asking about the form's first question: Why am I here? "Did you want to fill this out, or shall we as mother and daughter do it together?"

Miley answered by asking; "Don't you think we're here because we need some professional help? This constant sickness is stressful."

I nodded, saying, "I have needle-like pains shooting through my chest. Yes, we do. There's obviously problems." I had concluded that my problem was either bacteria or stress, and probably a combination of both that dated back to the 1983 blood transfusion lies. "I live in a place where I have no rights to effective antibiotics. I don't go to a doctor to be lied to, but they do lie to me, and that's one of my stress problems!"

An older, slender woman appeared. She wore her dark hair short, and a loose-fitting dark dress. Judging by her facial wrinkles, she was in her sixties. The dark-haired woman called my name. She introduced herself as the interviewing therapist. She and I walked into her office.

The first question that was on the form "Why am I here" was now on the therapist's lips.

Immediately I referred to the "God Visits" dream, which I had written down and a copy of which I held. "I'm in the process of interpreting this dream. I have searched for assistance, but the interpretation isn't yet completed. Only the dreamer can truly interpret their dream. The dream's accuracy devastates me," I said, while pulling out three of my husband's blood test papers, and one paper describing an antibiotic that was a good anti-tumor and anti-virus medicine. That medicine was housed in a medical chemotherapy

cupboard to be used only after the human tissue turned malignant.

I assumed that the therapist knew that the blood was like a road map as it flowed to the tissue. A normal white blood cell figure for my husband and me was about a six. So a ten figure would be too high. I spread Carl's 1994, 1995, and 1996 blood test result copies on the therapist's desk in order that she could clearly see the White Blood Cell Differential figures. The Basophil figure was raised 10 times higher than the normal-high-tolerance-level range. Although the blood tests did not include the word Myelocytes, they normally were stained with the Basophils. Therefore the basophil figure would include a disease marker.

First, I pointed to my husband's October 1994 blood test, saying, "Notice the Basophils range figure." I had written what the tolerance range should be right next to the range that was used. "The range that was used, has been raised 10 times higher than a normal high range should be. This 1994 blood test was taken when my husband Carl had a colon cancer surgery. At that time, the removed tumor was diagnosed as malignant, and no follow-up treatment was recommended. Carl left the hospital in 1994 without an antibiotic despite his blood test showing unusual cell activity."

Carl's 1994 blood test was the following:

TEST	RESULT	LOW-HIGH	(VARIATIONS)	PERSONALIZED
White Blood Cells	8.4	4.5-11.0	(4.5-10.0)	6
Platelet Count	285	140-400	(150-350)	225
Differential (Totals 100% of the white-blood-cell-size variations)				
Myelocytes 0 (a blood-disease indicator when in the blood).				
Neutrophils	68.7	30-80	(54-62)	59

Lymphocytes	16.3	20-60	(25-33)	30
Monocytes	12.9	2-20	(3-7)	5
Eosinophils	1.1	.01-5.00	(.01-3)	1
Basophils	.9	.01-5.00	(0-0.5)*	0.2

*Basophils high tolerance level. A 5% was used on the blood test instead of the suggested normal high of 0.5%.

Next, I showed the therapist Carl's 1995 blood tests, and pointed to the increased Basophils cell figure.

Carl's 1995 blood test was the following:

TEST	RESULTS	LOW-HIGH	(SHOULD BE)	PERSONALIZED
Myelocytes	0 (a blood-disease indicator)			
Neutrophils	68.5	30-80	(54-62)	59
Lymphocytes	20.2	20-60	(25-33)	30
Monocytes	8.2	2-10	(3-7)	5
Eosinophils	1.5	.01-5.00	.01-3)	1
Basophils	1.7	.01-5.00	(0-0.5)	.02

*The 1.7% was not flagged because the high tolerance level was again 5% instead of 0.75%. Again the laboratory figure had a 10 times the normal figure increase.

I proceeded to explain, "This 1995 blood test was done after I had called for 911 assistance, because Carl was having a breathing problem. The woman dream-character was the emergency room doctor. The emergency room doctor stated that she couldn't find any cause for my husband's breathing problem. Heart bacterial destruction

does not take place quickly."

I pointed out what the blood tests looked like when the dream characters appeared in reality. Both dream characters were doctors. The woman carrying the white blank 2'X1' sign appeared in 1995 and the man carrying the white blank 2'X1' sign appeared on May 15, 1996.

For a clearer explanation, I rewrote my husband's 1995 blood tests to merge the 10 times increase tolerance levels with the normal low and high tolerance levels. I began showing the therapist the abnormalities and how many of the white blood cells would have been flagged with the normal lab test figures, which were the following:

TEST	RESULT	LOW-HIGH	FLAG (Personal Figure)
White Blood Cells	9.3 H*		6.0
Myelocytes	0 (a blood-disease indicator)		
Neutrophils	68.5	54-62 H*	59
Lymphocytes	20.2	25-33 L*	30
Monocytes	8.2	3-7 H*	5
Eosinophils	1.5	.01-3.00	1
Basophils	1.7	.0-0.5 H*	.02

* Five blood tests figures should have been flagged, but weren't.

I proceeded to show the therapist the third blood test dated May 15, 1996 when the man carrying the white 2'X1' sign appeared, saying, "Notice the Basophils had disappeared. I wrote to England, and they use a similar medical system."

TEST	RESULT	RANGE	(BRITISH)	(MEAN)
White Blood Cells	10.2			6.0
Myelocytes	0 (a blood-disease indicator)			
Neutrophils	9.2 H	2.0-9.0	(2.4-6.2)	3.0
Lymphocytes	0.5	0.4-3.5	(1.1-3.3)	2.1
Monocytes	0.5	0.0-1.0	(0.14-0.7)	0.36
Eosinophils	0.0*	0.0-0.5	(0.02-0.3)	0.14
Basophils	0.0*	0.0-0.2	(0-0.08)	0.03

*The abnormal cell activity that was present had disappeared.

The doctor and the hospital's name appeared at the top of the May 15, 1996 blood-test page, which was the building next door to the Fox Clinic. So, I continued to explain why I felt that the altering of medical tests was human destruction! As I ranted about the two-year-noticeable-abnormal-cell-figure, Carl had completed two weeks of the cardiologist's recommended 6-week Gentamicin Sulfate USP protocol. The specialists should have been familiar with the fact that it had only a 10 to 12 day limitation.

The therapist asked, "Is the patient still alive?"

"Yes. Unfortunately under the system, he's a dead man." I placed my hand on the page identifying Carl's 1983 most effective antibiotic named Adriamycin. Adriamycin was also call Doxorubicin. It was an antibiotic isolated from cultures of mutant streptomyces.

"The 6-year old patent antibiotic was removed from general use and placed into the Hazardous Substance Data Bank by Copyright 1974-year Micromedex, Inc. The tumor fighting antibiotic became a part of a cancer-treatment chemotherapy protocol and had not been used as an antibiotic in the U.S. since 1974. I tried to think of an example of how limiting it was to limit antibiotic use to IV injections only. "Just the other day, I was putting the pump IV line, containing the antibiotic Penicillin G (of unknown origin to the patient), together and the line was filled with bubbles. I had to call the agency, who then called the visiting nurse, who then called back to tell me how to get the bubbles out."

The therapist jotted notes.

So, I continued to describe a century of withholding good medicines, beginning with the tuberculosis vaccine that was discovered in 1908, and never used in the United States. When a medical person said that the BCG vaccine was used in the United States and it wasn't, that person should have been called a medical liar. The same should go for antibiotics. In the 1960's, it was known that all cells mutated and that the mutated germs could be made into antibiotics. An example would be Adriamycin, that was made from mutated bacterium.

The therapist changed the subject by asking the form's next question: What kind of medications are you taking now?

I shrugged my shoulders, saying, "None."

I again changed the subject back to my concern over what I had called "Health Sabotage" in 1983 by pulling out my papers titled Blood Type Identification, saying, "Twice I had my blood drawn to get one. The second time I was told that it wasn't done under normal conditions, which was for a health test. Let me explain these antibodies to you."

I then showed the therapist the list of antibodies in the Blood Type Identification:

BLOOD TYPE: A2 ANTIBODIES: +DAT, S-, s+, K+k+, Fy a+, Fy b+, Jk a+, Jk b+.

Again the therapist fluffed her hand, "I know nothing about medicine," and she changed the subject back to the questionnaire. This time she asked about alcoholic problems.

"I'm an ex-alcoholic, my mother's a current alcoholic, my father is crazier than 'wh-oose-c-oo-w' (that's like the Madd Hatter in Alice in Wonderland), and my younger brother is more vain than the wicked witch in Snow White. I have an older brother, but he's kind-a normal."

My thoughts remained on how I was going to present my next subject. I have been complaining about blood-test alterations (the discrediting of disease markers) and the withholding of common-sense antibiotics for over two decades. My 1995 complaint to the Department of Licensing and Regulations about the raising of lab blood test 10 times what the figure should have been had appeared to fall upon deaf ears, until the known figures disappeared.

I had purchased a black Haitian voodoo hex doll from a mail order catalogue. The four voodoo pins and curse were extra, and not known to be as effective as one conjured personally. I was attending a writer's workshop when a member didn't know what a voodoo doll was. So, at the workshop, I showed the $6 purchased black wax doll. And I explained that my curse was directed at the medical liars. I believed that a medical liar was a Health Saboteur. Lying drug prescribers used the prescription drug law to deprive my husband and me of the right to the more effective antibiotics. My curse was very simple: "May your lies be like tattoos and printed all over your body. As the lies flow from your mouth, death drips from your lips. May God call up your dead! Their ghosts parade through your corridors, chanting: 'you prayed to give your brain to the human parasites. May you die the way you murdered'."

The Bible told about blood and anti-Christ. To me, a medical liar would be a Health Saboteur, so if God represented light and truth then the medical liar and the Anti-Christ represented darkness and lies. The phrase was simple: "The God that you speak is the God that you worship."

The therapist and I didn't seem to be talking about the same subjects. So, I asked her, "Do you know what a curse is?"

"A curse?"

"Yes, a curse," I repeated. "It never dawned on me that there are people who don't know what a curse is, even if that curse is staring them in the face."

The therapist glanced at her watch. My hour must have been almost over, as the therapist asked, "Shall I call in your daughter?"

"Sure," I replied.

Miley entered the room and sat in the chair next to me. The therapist explained her recommendations: "Your mother's thought are too scattered. We have a Monday-through-Friday-program with the hours of 9 a.m. to 3 p.m. to assist in her mental organization. (Money-wise that would be 6-hours x 5-days = 30 hours x $126-per-hour, making the cost $3,780 per week.) Your mother can have helpful prescription drugs and professional guidance to assist her in logically arranging her now-scattered thoughts."

I looked at Miley, maintaining my stance by saying, "I might as well date my book back to when your dad had his 1977 gallbladder surgery." The results were another noticeable untreated infection.

The therapist immediately shook her head, commenting, "This case is worse than I thought it is. If your mother began therapy tomorrow, it wouldn't be soon enough."

Miley nodded, "I'll try to do what I must do, the best I can."

The meeting was at a conclusion, so Miley left.

The interviewer – therapist and I walked to an area where a second receptionist sat. "This is where you will be checking in for treatment. Of course, I can't take you through the treatment area. We don't place our patients on display. You know how your husband is receiving medicines to make him better. Well, you will also be given medicines to make you better. Do you think that you're the only sane person?"

First I thought, "If I'm the only person who thinks that the withholding of good antibiotics and the altering of blood test levels was health sabotage, then my answer would have to be a yes." So I answered, "Yes. I am the only sane person in my book."

I creased my conversation to receive the therapist's reaction. I was annoyed with the interviewer who fluffed-off every medical question I asked. To me, health sabotage was a form of treason. Health Sabotage was the destruction of my country by promoting illness and medical misinformation. Treason used to be a concern to everyone who lived in the United States. By this time, I believed that medical treason, was to be either ignored or considered fashionable a century ago, when tuberculosis was the #1 disease killer. To condense one hour of conversation: a medical liar was a medical murderer!

The therapist replied, "Here you can work on your book five days a week between the hours of 9 a.m. to 3 p.m."

I asked, "And I'll also have lots of medical research books at my disposal?"

"Oh, yes. There will be other things for you to do, too."

Again, as we spoke, Carl had completed two weeks of the cardiologist's recommended 6-week protocol. The specialists should have been familiar with the fact that Gentamicin Sulfate only had a 10 to 12 day usage. The prescription drug over-dosing was present to the specialist, but not visible to the patient. Instead it was a "let-the- patient/medical customer beware" approach. Thus our $126-per-hour conversation had ended, so I left.

Instant Insanity

Chapter 16

Home From Clinic

June 11, 1996

On June 11, 1996 I had drove to the Miami Psychiatric Clinic in my husband's Uncle Lewis's 1989 Pontiac Sunbird. Carl's Uncle Lewis died in May 1994, and Carl was the estate's executor for the two heiresses: Maxine and Virginia. Therefore, there was a legal advisor that was aware of Carl's bacterial-produced heart disease and the recommended treatment protocol.

After returning home from the Miami clinic, I noticed that my husband was sitting in the family room demobilized. My thoughts were wondering what the connection was between his swollen feet and ankles and the difficult to detect bacterial-produced heart disease Endocarditis.

I tried to shift through the remnant items of reality that I overlooked. Those tiny details could hold information or directions as to where to go or what to do at the time of a real sickness.

Then Carl asked about my Miami Clinic visit. "Well," I replied, "it's a place that makes its money with human occupancy at $126-per-hour. They, too, work like human parasites, feeding upon the human brain. I was given the impression that their subjects are drained of money and life with drugs, if they don't smarten up and leave! The Clinic claims to do with medication what some people used to do with meditation."

When Miley returned home from work, she walked over to her dad to whisper: "The therapist said that mother should have begun psychiatric treatment yesterday."

I was standing at the kitchen sink, doing dishes, and listening to my husband and daughter conversation. Carl replied, "Well, we'll just have to put it on hold. I have to have somebody give me those IV's."

"Gee-e-e, dad, I can learn how to do that."

"That's all right, honey," Carl said while flipping his wrist and motioning with his hand for Miley to calm down. "I'll let your mother do it. Thank you for the offer."

All of a sudden both Carl and Miley stopped talking to look my way. I was under the impression that they were wondering if I had heard them!

"Yes, I hear you two whispering. The next time you make an appointment for me, make it with a real psychologist. Don't make it with a scavenger who feeds upon human stupidity. Make sure the person knows something about medicine and how medical lies affect people!"

Carl condensed the complete medical-physical and emotional situation: "Your problem is that you're hung up on Dr. McClarens calling you crazy."

"Well," I reminded Carl; "the day she called me crazy was the day that the ambulance transported you to another hospital. And furthermore, the hematologist lied about your being all right in six months! It took three years for your back surgery to heal!"

I believed that when a medical person lies, they should be called "the anti-Christ." The hematologist was using the prescription drug law to deliberately withhold antitumor/ antiviral antibiotics. By 1983 both the hematologist and the pathologist knew that they were transfusing tainted blood, and they were deliberately producing a contradiction. The contradiction was a damn lie! Somehow there was a relationship between the 1977 medical lies and the hematologist's 1983 medical lies. If the lies were noticed by the educational, medical, and psychological world in 1977, they had to be noticed by 1996 at the Miami Psychiatric Clinic.

Instant Insanity
Chapter 17
June 12, 1996

I know that when I became caught up in a dream, the dream often contained an abundance of reality. Somehow there was a relationship between the "God Visits" dream and my husband's dreaming that he died! There was something in both dreams that were more real than reality itself.

That night both my husband and I again had unusual dreams. First I'll tell mine.

I dreamt that I was sitting next to a large, dark, wood-grain desk. It was a sunny day surrounded by pleasant clouds. The office was outside; it had no walls. I had a steno pad in my left hand and a pencil in my right, while the dream's narrator was discussing the subject "The Mutated Theory". The theory contained three subjects: Brain, Genes, and Microorganisms. Each of the three subjects, when 100% synthetic, came under the same definition: a mutated deterioration.

I was desperately looking for information. Indeed, this was more than I had hoped to find.

"I'm impressed," I said, moving my head from the marvelous heavenly scene to look upon the person dictating the words.

A robust man dressed in a brown suit sat behind the desk. I stared at his face, trying to see the color of his eyes. Then I noticed that I was gazing into a vast sky with a few distant clouds painted in the background. I was awestruck that the kind speaker had no human eyes. So I slowly turned my head to the right. The sky extended into space. My eyes scanned across the vastness.

I looked down at my notes, as I heard the narrator say, "You stopped writing. You're going to need all this information."

Again I looked at the narrator's face. Poof! There was none. If it weren't for the brown suit, HE, the narrator, would have been invisible. It was then that I awoke.

If Gentamicin Sulfate USP was known to drug overdose halfway through the 6-week protocol, Carl's dream may have been warning him. The Gentamicin drug overdosing wasn't mentioned until July 3, 1996. Thus I came to the conclusion that if Gentamicin only had a 10-12 day normal recommendation, June 12, 1996 was the last day of a comfort zone for its use.

On June 12, 1996, I wrote down my husband's dream, which was the following:

Carl dreamt that he was walking down the streets of Rome. Italian music filled the air. He could see the historic buildings, some of which were thousands of years old. Carl noticed that several people, as well as he, were pushing an IV-stand as they walked down the street.

Then Carl met a stranger who had no IV. Carl stopped the man to ask "why no IV?"

The stranger replied, "I don't need one. My when-I-get-sick medicine is still in an easy-to-swallow pill form." Then the stranger told Carl that Carl didn't need an IV either.

Carl forgot that he lived in a different country and in a state where dictated drugs were the only ones provided. The old prescription drug law stated that a person could not receive antibiotics without a prescription. The patient had to take the antibiotic that the drug prescriber recommended, or receive nothing.

My husband woke in a hallucinatory state. Still dazed by the dream, Carl didn't recognize reality. He got up and went into the bathroom to remove the eighteen-inch-pic line that was inside his arm.

I woke at 6:00a.m. Carl was sitting at the kitchen table. I begin to gather the needed items for his 7:00a.m. Gentamicin sulfate IV, when I noticed that the pump Carl carried containing the penicillin G was missing. Normally, I would disconnect the penicillin G pump-continuous-flow IV and hook-up the gentamicin drip. After the drip IV was completed, I would then re-attach the pump IV line containing the penicillin G.

I sat down, saying, "You don't have your pump and your IV hook-up is g-o-n-e. I'm going to have an extremely difficult time attaching your next antibiotic dose."

Carl looked at his arm where the IV connection used to be and shrugged his shoulders, saying, "So, I'll go and get another one."

At this point, I knew that whatever I said was going to be wrong. "Okay. Then you do it."

Carl called several phone numbers, before he received instructional information stating that he should go to the hospital to receive another IV pic implant.

Carl and I drove to the building that was next door to the Fox Clinic; to have his new eighteen-inch-pic line inserted.

Several questionnaires had to be verbally filled out. Carl had a complaint about one: "My wife is going to have a nervous breakdown. Is there some way that these IV's can be made simpler? My wife knows nothing about medicine and medical procedure. The home-care people go too fast with their quick home-care instructions. Then when the instructions are given over the telephone, it's more nerve-wracking, and my wife becomes flustered."

When Carl and I were sitting alone waiting for Carl's new pic-line, the doctor who carried the blank white sign in the 1994 dream entered the room. It was the second time that the doctor, who was an internal medicine specialist, had appeared in Carl's medical reality. The specialist wasn't in the room to wish Carl well, so Dr. Woodbury did prior to

Carl's first 1983 cancer. At that point in time, the gentamicin became an over-used antibiotic.

Carl and I were unaware of what the specialists knew, so we continued to complain about the IV-pic removal. I complained to Carl about his complaining: "I'm getting chest pains. I'll probably have a heart attack before I have a nervous break down."

Carl's dream could have been saying something similar to "You don't need any more Gentamicin treatments". Often I assume that because a physician prescribes a medicine, the physician is using his medical knowledge. It had never dawned on me that a physician would prescribe a medicine that the medical cult would make the most money on, and then never check the blood for the prescription medicine's effects. Carl's doctors probably did check the blood, but ignored the gentamicin toxicity, which should have appeared.

When I compared the attitude of the legal liars "Lie and leave the people die, never tell the truth" and the style of the medical liars with the 1993 terrorist bombing of the World Trade Center, I believed that more people could die to medical evildoers than bombs or bullets. At the time of the 1993-World-Trade-Center-bombing the American Spirit were known in South America and other parts of the world as Organ Thieves. Unnoticed bacterial infections were destroying body parts, such as the heart, lungs, and kidneys.

Also at the time of the 1993-World-Trade-Center-bombing, every cardiologist knew that Gentamicin Sulfate USP was a short-term (10 to 12 day) antibiotic and that it would drug over-dose on the recommended 6-week protocol. The placing of too-many germs in a vaccine and medical drug over-dosing created a larger medical business.

Carl had his new eighteen-inch-pic line installed in his arm and we returned home. That night, I decided to sleep in the basement so that I would hear Carl moving better. During the night Carl woke. I could hear him walking around, and also with a thud noise with each step. I went upstairs. Carl was dragging his portable IV machine that was attached to his new 18-inch pic line implant.

I was shocked at the sight and said, "You are supposed to carry the IV gadget!"

Carl looked at the floor and IV machine gadget, and said, "I thought I was walking the dog. I must be still asleep."

The nightmares continued. A few weeks later (before the end of the 6-week protocol) my husband asked that I drop him off in the local field so that he could crawl off to die like a dog.

The drug of choice, Gentamicin Sulfate USP, remained as the drug of choice on a 6-week protocol, and again created additional problems in January 2002. If a cardiologist never noticed that the drug of choice drug over-dosed, nobody else was supposed to notice.

Instant Insanity
Chapter 18

June 28 to June 30, 1996

On June 28, 1996, Carl asked me to drive him to the local field, drop him off, and let him crawl off like a dog to die. Meanwhile, politicians had passed laws to legalize punishment of the people who carried out the medical victim's dying wish. It was obvious that Carl would die, and I would be punished. So, I asked Carl to call his doctor. The doctor told my husband to go to the hospital emergency room (ER).

Carl couldn't get up. I called my neighbors Betty, Robert, Andrea, and Chris to help me get Carl the 20 steps to the pickup truck parked outside the back door. We arrived at the ER, and Carl was helped inside, while I parked the truck. The ER doctor knew at first sight what Carl's problem was. The talented doctor ghoul placed one hand over the other as his words came out: "You need a new heart valve!" The specialist's eyes flashed like the ring of a cash register!"

Again, there was no available attorney to question the poisonous effect of the drug-of-choice used on a 6-week protocol (it would kill the patient, before it cured)! I felt that if the Department of Licensing and Regulations knew who the "They" people were, they should have informed the public decades ago. I left the hospital to go home to puke!

The next day, I returned. I entered Carl's room at the same time as cardiologist Dr. Jackson, and Internal Medicine specialist Dr. Atkins. The two specialists were surprised at Carl's condition. Dr. Atkins stated: "First I've heard of this!"

Then both specialists pretended to be surprised at Carl's dying appearance! They chatted among themselves, each stating that on Carl's last visit he was able to walk into their offices with no problems!

So, I asked Carl if he wanted to die! Carl said "no".

When a specialist prescribes a test that would kill the patient, it's not easy to say

"No" without causing ill feelings. I had heard that the little camera used to check the heart would cause an instant heart attack if the patient had a blockage or a hole in the heart. I would expect that the specialist knew that, too! As the specialists spoke, there were two holes in Carl's heart caused by the bacterial damage!

I used my husband's medical doctoring and medical records as an example of why I would like to choose my own antibiotics to doctor me! I have one question to ask each medical specialist: "Why was the lying about every blood tests the most important thing in their medical career?"

Instant Insanity
Chapter 19
July 1-4, 1996

July 1-4, 1996, which was a part of Carl's hospitalization from July 1 to 22, 1996 after being transferred by ambulance.

In May 1996, my husband, Carl, had a bacterial-produced difficult-to-detect hole

in his heart. The antibiotics of choice were Gentamicin sulfate USP and

penicillin G sodium chloride. By the end of June, Carl was in extremely

bad shape. Apparently Carl had been treatment drug over-dosed, and there

were several holes in his heart. On June 28, 1996 both Carl's specialist

entered Carl's hospital room. One specialist lied and the other swore that

the lie was true. They wanted to do a heart cauterization. I felt that

both specialists knew that my husband had a hole in his heart, and that if
the camera became hung up in the hole in the heart, the
test would have killed Carl. So, I asked my husband, "Do you want
to die?"

Carl shook his head to say "No!"

Therefore, I would NOT sign for the test. After a few days of hem-in-and-
haw-in, Carl was moved by ambulance.

On July 1, 1996, my daughter and I drove to the hospital. We looked for Carl who was someplace in the heart intensive-care unit. We wondered around the hospital until we found him. While daughter and I were in the room, I noticed several hanging IV bags. One plastic package was an antibiotic called Penicillin G with sodium chloride. The Gentamicin Sulfate drug-of-choice was nowhere around.

The Penicillin IV reminded me of two things: first the 1994 dream titled
"God Visits", then the 1983 reality about how penicillin used for a
gram-negative infection was a joke. During Carl's 1983 cancer treatment it
was a hematologist joke that some infection penicillin won't affect. It was
an absolute joke as the hematologist told Carl and I about a doctor treating

a Hodgkin's disease patient with penicillin, when it was obvious that a
different antibiotic was clearly needed.

Later that day, Carl had a medical test that was something like an
echocardiogram. The test had a probe that was run down Carl's throat and
maneuvered as close to his heart as possible. I was also told that Carl had
a Coronary Angiography, a Radiographic (C's. grafts, IMA, Aortogr) and an
Aortography. The big medical words I listed were used on the medical
billing. We received a copy of the bills and not a copy of the medical
tests. A separate payment would have to be made if copies of the tests were
requested to go with the billing records. (I noticed that the medical
computer is set up to omit letters and, even numbers if it used them.) A
person or Medicare could NOT compare the bill with the test, if no test
copies were received.

After Carl's echocardiogram, a doctor had sat down with my daughter and
myself. He drew a diagram to show the microbe infection damage done on Carl's heart. First the doctor explained the infection damage to the upper left

side while drawing marks. Then he drew an X marking where an abscess had
   formed on the right ventricle. Carl needed surgery to remove the infection
   from the infected and damaged areas.

After the doctor left, daughter and I discussed the heart problem. "Your
   dad has two infections that produced two holes in his heart."

"No mother," daughter corrected, "the doctor said an infection on the left
   and an abscess on the right."

"An abscess is an infection," I tried to explain that to me Carl's heart
   had more than one kind of deterioration. The damage description was
   produced by more than one kind of microbe germ parasite.

"The doctor said," daughter reiterated the doctor's words, "Infection," and
   she flipped her left hand palm-side up. Then she pointed out the word
   "Abscess," and flipped her right hand palm-side up, continuing, "If an
   abscess was an infection, he would have said that an abscess was an

infection. He didn't say that. So, do us both a favor and use only the
doctor's words."

On the same day, several other family members entered Carl's room. The
other family members had been told that Carl's infection was gone. Nothing
was said to daughter and I about the infection being gone. Daughter and I
were under the impression that they had to surgically remove the infection
when cutting into Carl's heart.

Antibiotics have been a joke since the 1983 hematologist joked about
treating Hodgkin's disease with penicillin. Now it was a joke about how
Gentamicin Sulfate USP drug over-dosed in 2-3 weeks. It was a short-term
antibiotic. Yet, American Heart Association and The Heart
specialist had called it "the drug of choice" on a 6-week protocol for
almost two decades, knowing that it would drug over-dose.

The next day, daughter and I entered Carl's room and noticed that Carl was
hallucinating. Daughter and I were amused to watch Carl hallucinate looking

for his screwdriver. He wanted to open the door without breaking locks or
destroying the doorknob. "Find my screwdriver and remove the hinges and
take the door completely off," Carl demanded.

Our conversation ended when a doctor entered the room. He introduced
himself as an Internal Medicine-Infectious Diseases. Immediately, I
thought, "Another drug specialist with another plan of medical expertise."

So I asked the doctor about the old method of using the Electron Microscope
to take a blood cell photo. The Electron Microscope was used back in the
1970's. The super-enlarged photo identified various pathogenic infections
that were carried in the blood before the microorganisms settled on a tissue
site.

"I never heard of it," said the doctor.

"You never heard of an Electron Microscope?"

"I-I've heard of the Electron Microscope," the doctor corrected, "I've never
heard of it being used on the blood. In Pathology, we use it ONLY on the

tissue."

My memory flashed to a time-slot in 1975. In 1975, Carl and I lived next

door to an electron-microscope repairman. He was selling his microscope

that was about three-feet-tall, between four-or-five-feet-long and at least

two-feet-wide, and he asked me, "Would you like to buy my microscope for

$250?"

"Yes. But for $250, I have to ask Carl. If you'll take $200, I'll drag it

next door now and worry about what Carl says later!"

The neighbor wasn't in a bargaining mood. So I wandered home to tell Carl

and began rearranging the laundry room. The microscope needed to be by a

water supply. The machine ran hot and was water-cooled. Meanwhile the

neighbor and Carl were talking. The neighbor was telling Carl that the

machine cost him $20-an-hour to operate. He also showed Carl all the

pictures that he had taken: dirt, fly legs, and many interesting little

back-yard critters.

Now in 1996 twenty-one years later, I looked at the doctor and then Carl, thinking: "Dear, you need a blood cell photo. You should have bought that

microscope. It's common knowledge that many pathogenic microorganism

infections have been detected in the blood with those photos!"

The 1996 reality was that Carl needed a heart surgery to remove the

existing infection. Carl was scheduled to have his heart surgery the next

day at 6:30 a.m. The next day the 6:30 a.m. surgery was postponed until

7:30 a.m. Then at 7:30 a.m., the surgeon came to speak with me.

To perform a surgery knowing that the medical client would not survive would

be tacky for all parties concerned. The surgeon did not recommend the

surgery. There was less than a 10% chance of survival with the surgery and

0% with the infection remaining.

I, immediately, thought that using an antibiotic that was known to drug

over-dose after a 2-3 week usage, on a 6-week protocol was disgusting. All

the antibiotics that were used were known not to be the most effective that

fought the known infection. Carl's best-known effective antibiotics were

Doxorubicin (also called Adriamycin) and Bleomycin. They were in the cancer
   building next door, and not to be used unless malignant tissue was
      identified.

As I spoke with the surgeon, I made the decision to cancel the heart surgery.

My decision was based on two facts: first, Carl's microbe germ-parasite
   infection remained. Why so many family members were told that the infection
      was gone was a puzzle? And second reason was that Carl's most known effective antibiotics that were Adriamycin and Bleomycin that were used in 1983 and were not going to be used.

While waiting for death, I examined the Gentamicin Sulfate USP antibiotic
   closer.

Gentamicin was an old antibiotic. Originally Gentamicin was made from
   micromonosporal and was active against gram-positive and gram-negative
      bacteria and protozoa. It had many formulas none of that contained sulfur.

Where did the sulfur come from?

Initials used in chemistry:

C - carbon Cl - chlorine H - hydrogen

K - potassium N - nitrogen Na - sodium

O - oxygen S - sulfur

Name Formula

Gentamicin A1 - $C_{18} H_{36} O_{10} N_4$

Gentamicin A2 - $C_{17} H_{33} O_9 N_3$

Gentamicin A3 - $C_{18} H_{36} O_{10} N_4$

Gentamicin A4 - $C_{19} H_{36} O_{11} N_4$

Gentamicin B - $C_{19} H_{38} O_{10} N_4$

Gentamicin B1 - $C_{20} H_{40} O_{10} N_4$

Gentamicin C1 - $C_{21} H_{43} O_7 N_5$

Gentamicin C1a - $C_{19} H_{39} O_7 N_5$

Gentamicin C2 - $C_{20} H_{41} O_7 N_5$

Gentamicin X - $C_{19} H_{38} O_{10} N_4$ (Cooper, Waitz, a German Patent in 1972)

In the 1980's the chemical substance sulfate was added to Gentamicin.

The new Gentamicin Sulfate USP drug formula fact that it was a short-term

antibiotic (2-3 week) information was unavailable to the medical consumer.

And the American Heart Association recommended Gentamicin Sulfate

USP as a "Drug of Choice" on a 6-week protocol for the treatment of

endocarditis, a heart disease caused by bacteria colonizing in heart and

producing deterioration.

After I made my morning surgery cancellation decision, the surgeon

suggested that a group decision was the normal conventional step.

He suggested that the families gather, and went to make a few phone calls.

I went to the pay telephones in the main lobby. I couldn't get the pay

phone to work. I tried and tried with no luck. Finally, I gave up on the

telephones. I was walking back to Carl's room, when from a distance,

I saw my younger brother, Elijah, and Carl's son Duane walking into the

waiting room.

"Wow, they must be psychic," I thought, as I ran to catch up to them.

I was surprised to see that the meeting room was filled with relatives.

There were at least seven of us. Both of Carl's sisters were unable to

make the decision-making meeting.

The surgeon and another physician entered the room. The subject again was

the canceling of Carl's heart surgery. This time the surgery cancellation

was presented to all present family members who were previously told that

Carl's infection was gone. No one could understand one thing: If the

infection were gone, why would the surgery be cancelled? A second

discussion was that the Gentamicin Sulfate USP had produced a metabolism in

Carl's body that caused his kidneys to shutdown. Both doctors knew that

Carl was Gentamicin Sulfate USP drug over-dosed, and they actually stated

it to the family.

I wanted to ask about the echocardiogram's colors that were often used as

toxic information. Most distinct was the red that showed up on Carl's

colored heart test, but then I thought about the family's probable reply,

"Kristine, you're so heartless!"

To me, the definition of heartless was the deliberate withholding of

effective antibiotics and permitting the microbe infection to damage organs.

The family had been lied to since the grandfather's tuberculosis

treatment.

Again that afternoon, Carl's heart surgery was cancelled. This time all the

present family members called it off. The subject was "Why do a surgery

when the patient would not live?"

The surgeon had a five-day vacation scheduled from this day until the following Monday. There was no reason for him not to go, so the surgeon

left for vacation.

After everybody went home, I remained. I walked around the hospital

grounds, looking for Hospital Ghosts, spirits who had died before their

time. To my surprise, there was an old tuberculosis sanatorium. The

hospital's back door remained a tuberculosis sanatorium. A vision appeared

of an old photo snap-shot of a doctor suffocating his tuberculosis child

patient. The image was embroidered in the threads of time and woven into

eternity. It was a portrait of an evil doctor that would kill his patient

before ever looking for or using a tuberculosis vaccine.

If the Bible says, "For the life of the flesh is in the blood", then the

evil doctor would be similar to the anti-Christ who would be saying the

opposite, which would be "Suck the blood from the flesh...Blood means

nothing!" An example would be the electron microscope used on

the tissue only, and not used on the blood that feed the flesh.

I returned inside disappointed that I didn't met with any real ghosts.

The next day July 4, 1996, I walked into Carl's room to discover that he had been placed on a respirator, also referred to as a ventilator. The respirator baffled me. During the night, I had a dream about a new addition to the room, but I expected something to be hanging on the wall. My first thought was that a machine replaced common-sense medicine. The withholding of $25 worth of effective antibiotics would produce a $250,000 heart surgery. Since the surgery was cancelled, the respirator was a

symbol of a picture of a simple business mode.

Again, I left the room to search for the hospital ghosts who died because

of heart disease. A hospital ghost would be best described as an

apparition. The body died before its time and the spirit lingered.

After the "God Visits" dream, I had asked about the Blood Type

Identification Card. Antibiotics and blood tests had a lot to do with heart

disease. The hospital ghosts could also be described as metaphors in

relationship to blood antibodies: "they are there and if you look, you will

see."

A business that withholds effective antibiotics in order to have a large

return customer clientele would also have a collection of die-before-your-time ghost. Again, I walked around the hospital's large red brick complex building sections, looking for

deceased heart patients, but all I could find were the tuberculosis spirits.

Not far from the main entrance was a historic brick and gray mortar

sign: Sanitarium, A 1913D.

The sign intrigued me. So I pulled out my tape measure and placed it on

the 2'x3' rectangular block. Then I heard haunting screams. I looked

around to see from where the noise came. There were buildings and a few

people moving about. I looked around, and there was nothing making that

kind of a sound. I placed my ear to the old mortar sign. Yes, the sounds

were from inside the 1913-dated mortar sign. I looked closer. The cement

pores were filled with ancestry spirits and each held an aura of medical

secrets. Then all of a sudden ghosts were flying out from the pitted hollows

within the cement and from the bottom square in-between the number 3 and the letter D at the bottom of the sign. The ghosts were moving too quickly and

were too numerous to count karma.

Finally, three ghosts each wearing a cowboy hat stopped to chat. To whom

they were speaking, I couldn't clearly tell. I found the conversation

interesting, so I eased-dropped.

The first ghost was wearing a white cowboy hat with a black 3x3-inch paper

sign with the #1 tucked in the center. He had died sometime between the

year 1914 and 1919. The ghost was a patient at the sanitarium and he died

from a chlorine overdose. Judging from his conversation, back in the

pre-war era, people were used as guinea pigs for the chemical effects that

could be expected from the chemical warfare substances used on the First

World War enemy. The ghost wore his white hat like someone who was wearing

a job. He felt that he was patriotic, and that his death was for a good

cause. Then the ghost sounded as if he was arguing with an invisible

spirit, by saying, "The guy in the black hat doesn't agree with me."

I looked around and saw no one wearing a black hat. Again the ghost
referred to the invisible spirit. "You have to watch out for the guy in the
black hat. He does his job very well."

My attention then turned to the second ghost who wore a blue cowboy hat
with a white 3x3-inch sign with the #3, also tucked in the center. He, too,
was a patient and he died around 1939 from a chlorine overdose. He felt
that he was victimized by the again government funded secret chemical
testing. After all, it had been twenty years after the chemical overdose
was established. His tone wasn't as pleasant as the one wearing the white
hat. He called his doctors a cult, who claimed that they could wave a magic
wand.

The ghosts disappeared and I again returned inside the hospital
disappointed that I didn't find any heart disease deceased spirits.

Instant Insanity
Chapter 20
July 1-3, 1996

Three Dreams

For three consecutive nights three different dreams appeared. In my large purse setting next to me was the black voodoo hex doll and the four voodoo pins that I had with me on June 11, 1996; also in my purse was a book titled "1995 Physicians' Desk Reference".

The first night, I dreamt that I was inside a dark tunnel beneath the ground. It was like an old mining shaft. The mining shaft's vehicle in which I sat was operated by gravity and had no brakes. It ran down the already-mined tunnel on the present built tracks. Directly in front of me was a handle bar. On the vehicle there was a chrome-plated metal-tube handle bar soldered at both ends. The seat was close to the bar, enabling me to comfortably hold on. As I started to turn my head to look at the seat in back of me and at the rest of the vehicle, the speed accelerated. The movement jolted me to look forward and I tightly gripped the handle bar. Every now and then daylight would appear as if the sun reflecting upon the rock-supported walls. The brief burst of light immediately let me know that I was riding down a coal mineshaft in a vehicle that had no brakes. The light gave several meanings simultaneously: it let me guess 15-20 mph as the approximate speed, then wonder if the vehicle and I would hit a rock wall...the purpose and destination would be answered at the end of the trip.

Half way through the tour, there was no more light. The moving vehicle never stopped. It continued the downward, rocking ride. The narrow passage swerved to the left, then to the right, then made another sharp left turn. For a brief moment, I didn't think the vehicle was going to make the corner, but the vessel knew every inch of the tunnel and the black passage that stood straight ahead. The vehicle began to slow down where the man-made tracks ended at rock wall; the complete design was to crash into the wall. As I watched the rock approach, it turned into a large dark spot...like a burst of darkness. The rock became a part of the underground cave tunnel. It was like an addition to the man-made mineshaft and additional tracks were placed. I woke surprised that the vehicle didn't collide with the wall... it had gone through it!

The following night, a second dream vivid dream appeared. The dream brought with it a presentation of an eye diagram, and a narrative voice was discussing the eyes. "The white eye part will change color."

I worked my memory, thinking about a known subject: Carl's eyes were blue.

The dream began to point to the eye diagram. The display was like a computer lighting up the area discussed. It lit a gray haze overshadowing the blue. The dream's mannerism presented a conclusion as it continued describing <u>things</u> of death. It was presenting the known and established signs about death that a person already knew: a dead thing decays, death has a distinct odor and color.

The third night, I dreamt that I had walked into Carl's hospital room. As I entered Carl's room, something eye-catching and interesting was hanging on the right wall. I stopped and walked over to the item that looked like a newly hung picture frame. As I approached the unusual item to examine it, Carl sat up in his hospital bed. Both his wrist tie-downs were removed and Carl was sitting up under his own power, but he didn't open his mouth and he looked like a zombie. For a moment, I was doubly shocked: first at what I saw on the wall, and second that a doomed man sat up.

The way the dream described "doomed" was that once a person was entrapped inside this medical system…the system was designed NOT to survive.

Medical Patriotism

The dream gave a definition of a medical system designed Not To Survive.

We are a group of people who unlike any other country do NOT clutter our life with pariotism. As an individual, we know that we have a bureaucracy government who does NOT care about its people. Therefore, the bureaucracy has great influence on something that a "normal" person should have. The 'average" person must have forgotten that a bureaucracy is a group of people who make a government work or fail. So, when someone says: "You lost the 'cold war'. All that's left of the 'cold war' is the victory's name to be placed in history book print. The only reason the 'Victory's' name does not appear yet, is that the 'cold war' victory winners wish the United States assistance in the destruction of its allies before the 'big war' begins".

The bureaucracy has chose "legalism" as an excuse to kiss the "devil's feet", by placing restrictions on drugs, and their improper use. Also, during the Cold War, the infiltration of false drugs was replaced with the More Effective ones. As for myself, I am irate to think that government laws are forcing me to use the "wrong" drugs, and the local doctors are not tell their patients what countries the patients should go to in order to receive the "more effective" medicines.

Instant Insanity
Chapter 21
July 4-9, 1996

July 4-9, 1996, which is a part of Carl's hospitalization from

July 1–22, 1996 after being transferred by ambulance. The hospital ghosts care more and share more truth than the living.

After I noticed that my husband was placed on a ventilator on July 4, 1996, I was sitting next to Carl's bed to watch him die because of improperly treated bacterial infection. All of a sudden, a rude hospital executive-type lady approached me with new papers to be signed. Her manner was that she stomped into Carl's intensive care room and she was irRitated with everyone around, including me. Again, I was signing for Carl's heart surgery. I signed with pen in one hand, and the words on my lips: "If you think that I'm paying for this, then get ready to take me to court!"

The rude hospital lady stomped off with her signed paper, and I returned to my position of watching Carl die.

The next day I was in the hospital waiting room, pouring myself a cup of coffee when a familiar-looking elderly woman entered. I guessed her age to be in the late sixties. I had seen her walking pass Carl's room on the way to her husband who also was in intensive care. We made introduction, then began to chat. Betty's husband had recently had an artificial heart valve replacement, and it wasn't properly holding. Betty's husband was back in the hospital because the valve was leaking. Betty and I had one thing in common…any surgery using anything artificial weren't going to work! Betty's husband was on Medicare and they would pay for her Carl's hospitalization no matter what was done, and Medicare would never ask for any medical records where the hospital bill and medical test could be compared! A simple product paid for would be a product received. That kind of medical philosophy would date back to when the United States funded money looking for a tuberculosis (TB) vaccine when TB was the #1 disease killer in the USA? The federal fund-maker-grants forgot to ask that a product paid-for be a product received!

Personally, I would have preferred to have the known effective antibiotics, than to wait for a cadaver to fall from the sky. Medical evils have been present in the United States; I noticed the tuberculosis vaccine dilemma when I spoke with the tuberculosis hospital ghosts.

My thoughts began wondering. As I spoke with Betty, I also wondered how a medicine practitioner that withheld effective antibiotics could call their job humanity. To me that kind of medical person would be a heartless money-seeking human animal! So I spoke very cautiously with the elderly woman. Betty said, "They tell me to go home."

I nodded, saying, "They tell me that, too. But, why go home? If I were at home, I'd be wishing that I was here."

"Me, too," Betty agreed.

My younger brother Elijah and Carl's sister Joan stopped to visit. The three of us entered Carl's room. Joan commented: "I don't see Carl's hernia."

In 1994, Carl thought he pulled something when he was painting the eves, which was done at a time prior to his second tumor-produced cancer, (this same house area is now where new bees now have moved). The 1996 intensive-care nurse removed the sheets so that the three family members could examine Carl's hernia.

"Oh," I said, "look there are two Band-Aids placed in a cross-position. There an incision was made; maybe they fixed the hernia. It was a small one."

"No," all three nurses (two family members were nurses), "replied."

Again I pointed to the two Band-Aids, saying, "That's where the hernia was!"

The subject was discontinued. Both relatives left and there was a shift change.

The intensive care nurse and I watched the dialysis machine clog. Carl's body would jerk, as if having mini strokes while the dialysis machine would spit and spurt. It was common for bacterial-produced heart disease patients to have bacterial-produced strokes. The bacteria that grow around the heart and valve would break loose and travel, by the blood, to the brain. Sunday evening, July 7, 1996, the surgeon Dr. Samurson returned from vacation. To his surprise Carl was still alive, and the nurse told Dr. Samurson about the dialysis machine. So, I thought that I would add the fact that Carl's body was jerking as if having mini-strokes!

Then, I thought that I would be helpful and remove all other surprises by saying, "You are to speak with the family tomorrow."

Dr. Samurson asked, "Oh, really; what am I suppose to say?"

"I don't know," I replied, "they didn't give me a copy of the script. You are to speak with the family before Carl's tomorrow scheduled surgery."

The doctor asked no more questions. I could see by his eyes that he wasn't prepared to either speak with the family or prepared for a surgery.

On July 9, 1996, a cadaver had fell from the sky, and the heart surgery began. It was known that an infection and an abscess vastly destroyed Carl's heart. The surgeon used his art to great perfection opening Carl's chest (I guess they do it with an electric saw…just like a cook would cut open a chicken). Then he pulled out the heart, and chopped off the bacteria infected part. The cadaver's heart part that fell from the sky was used to replace the bacterial damage. The surgeon didn't need the complete heart only enough to replace the bacterial damaged area, which was either a quarter or a third. I wasn't there, but it would have been interesting. Meanwhile, I kept wondering why the known effective antibiotics were NOT used, in place of the sulfate garbage that was known to drug over-dose halfway through the recommended protocol.

The surgery was over. Bum-m-m-e-r. Unfortunately, there was leakage. So the surgeon had to reopen Carl's chest and do a few more stitches, then stuff the heart part back inside. After again wiring the chest shut and closing the incision, the leak was gone. The blood pump was turned on and the heart was zapped. The patient came back to life. The surgery was a success, but we (the medical specialist and myself) knew that the infection remained, while the rest of the family members had been told that the infection was gone. A lie had always been known as the opposite of truth. What would have been called the Mad Scientist, was now called surgically removing common bacteria infection and lying about withholding effective antibiotics as you do it.

After the surgery, Dr. Samurson spoke with the family. The doctor mentioned that Carl's heart was enlarged, and that he might have had a stroke. There was a problem on Carl's right side. How sever was yet to be seen.

The next day Carl recovered. The respirator was removed and he began to speak: "Get down! Get down! You're going to get shot!"

"No honey," I replied, "I not going to crawl around on the floor. They think that I'm crazy enough."

It was as if Carl had a split personality. Carl must have received a 75-year old person's heart. From the way he was speaking, it must have been from someone who was living in England during the Second World War. After spending one-hour at the Psychiatric Clinic (June 11, 1996) the month prior, I replied, "Why do you think that I'll be getting shot?"

"There's a war outside. Didn't you notice the bombs exploding and the gunfire blasting? Why did you come in here? I thought that you got away. Now, you're going to be a prisoner, too."

Immediately, I detected a slight hallucination problem. As other family members came to visit, I told them that Carl was hallucinating and not to be surprised at anything said. I started doing more reading and found in a nursing book a condition that was called "Sundowning, which was drug-produced."

The word sundown syndrome came from the sunset. In the drug world, it's a condition called "when the sun goes down the patient comes alive." Many drugs like steroids, sedatives, tranquilizers, sulfates, chlorides, and morphine produced an irregular heartbeat. I noticed that the irregular heartbeat showed up on the heart monitor.

As I read over the drug list, I thought that maybe Carl had every one of them. It surprised me that the family would be told that the infection was gone, and yet not be told that Carl was hallucinating. Since Carl was executor to his Uncle Lewis's estate, the hallucinating was a concern to Carl's mother. She had contacted the attorney who was handling the estate to change executors. Normally endocarditis heart patients in this shape do NOT live.

The hallucinations were daily and with every item that entered the room. Carl's sister had purchased a small planter with two-12-inch balloons that had the printed words "get well." The planter was placed against the back wall on a shelf. The balloons bounced with the air conditioner blowing.

I entered the room and Carl asked whom the two men were that were standing in the corner. "They came into my room last night. One has on a black cowboy hat, and the other is wearing a brown one. The two men have been standing there for hours and whispering. I can't hear them, and I find their whispering annoying. Who are they?"

I looked. The two men had disappeared, but their whispered words remained pasted all over the back wall. Death, a figuration of reality, was wearing the black cowboy hat and gathering his future prospects.

Death was speaking to an elderly man's spirit who was wearing the brown cowboy hat: "This is where the big bucks stopped."

The elderly man's body was like Carl's—a medical customer...only he was on Medicare. My first guess what that the elderly man resided in the room a few door down the hall. Now he was wearing the brown cowboy hat and having a conversation with Death...And Death was not giving out a bunch of lies. From the whispered words, I gathered that the subject was that the elderly man was Betty's husband and the medical customer in need of the cadaver's heart part first.

The apparition who wore the brown cowboy hat must have had a doctor that lied about the cadaver. The ghost who wore the black cowboy hat must have been the Death figure that the tuberculosis ghosts were talking about. So now Death was telling the apparition that appeared as Betty's husband the truth: "The hospital would not had been paid for the ambulance ride from nor would they had been paid for the nine day intensive care visit, if a surgery was not done."

What puzzled me about Carl's describing the whispering two figures was that according to the ghosts, spirits, or whatever they were, who said, "When you see Death, watch out."

I took that warning to mean that your own death wasn't far away. Carl saw the figure wearing the black hat, which meant to me Carl's death, too, was probably not far into the future.

I changed the subject and pointed to the balloons, saying, "You're sister…"

Before I finished my sentence, Carl interrupted. "God damn that's not my sister!"

"No. No, it's not. They're balloons."

Carl's face saddened. "You mean there's nobody there."

"Just balloons."

By 1996, the medical people knew that in 1994 a hospital laboratory had raised laboratory blood test figures as high as 10X's what the normal figure should have been. And by 1996, all the medical people were saying that the lab's increased figures had no affect identifying common bacterial blood infections.

Instant Insanity
Chapter 22

July 22, 1996

In the "God Visits" dream, the fourth person carrying the 1994 sign was a shadow. God meant many things to many people. I believed that God meant truth.

The "God Visits" dream took place at the time of my husband's 1994 colon cancer tumor surgery. Again, the tumor was caused by a tumor-producing pathogen. Again, no antitumor antibiotics were prescribed. Also at the time of the dream, specialists had placed Gentamicin Sulfate USP (a 10 to 12 day antibiotic) on a 6-week protocol, knowing that it would have no complaining survivors!

The dream had encouraged me to take Carl's "Blood Type Identification Card" and to ask the doctor about all the antibodies. The 1994 doctor looked at the card and stated that all the antibodies remained with that person forever.

In Carl's case, the antibodies disappeared two years later. In two years, my husband had a bacterial-produced heart disease appear, and he was at St. Joseph Hospital. At the front of the Hospital was a statue of the religious icon St. Joseph, which I believed to represent "truth" and medical lies were flying all around the building. On July 20, 1996, it was a warm, sunny day. So, I had Carl get into a wheel chair and I took him outside. We walked passed the cement 1913 sign and around the building. It was a long walk to the opposite side where a cement sign dated "1994" appeared.

When I saw the sign, I asked, "Who is your god?"

The sunlight was completely blocked with dark clouds. Over the hospital a large nimbus cloud with a face appeared. The dark cloud said: "I am god dam, god dam I am the prince of lies. You will follow me to your grave!"

As soon as the word "grave" was said, I could hear a quivering chant "lie for me, die for me". There was a group of people in back of me. It scared me to death. I didn't dare turn around.

The group walked single file passed me. Somehow, I knew that they were going to the god-like statute to gather. Each person that walked pass walked like a zombie, yet, looked like a normal living person.

I immediately formed the conclusion that when a country's lawmakers produced laws that would destroy truth and create destruction, the country would sickly die.

Again the "God Visits" dream:

As I slept, I could visualize my dreamself. I was dressed in a black turtleneck with matching black slacks. A black bandanna covered my hair. I was dressed as a thief going to a masquerade party. I didn't know that it was a Pirate's Carnival Fest until I arrived. Anyway, I appeared, also, as the person that was following behind like a television cameraperson who was recording the movie shot.

I followed, hoping that my dreamself would lead me to the disappeared Adriamycin that was a known antitumor/antiviral antibiotic. All of a sudden my dreamself stopped halfway up the hospital hall. The dream's narrator informed that the party was through the left wall and one floor up. My dreamself then turned to the left and proceeded to walk through the left wall.

Again I followed. Poof…The scene behind the wall changed to darkness. It was black on the wall's backside. As my dreamself transformed to slither through the cracks, I, too, followed. Soon I was on the other side and one-floor-up at the back of the room at the pirate's party fest. At the front of the room, the complete left wall was covered with white medicine cabinets, making musical sounds. I was standing in back of the room watching and listening to the pirate's music fest. The room was filled with firm-foot-stomping rhythm of power and wealth to a pirate's song. It was an interesting tune of folly and play. There was melodious whisper behind each white door that sounded like a humming chorus, "I am your god". Meanwhile, each cupboard door pompously warbled its own chorale verse: "A thief has his wealth, plus the wealth that he stole." The second cupboard door joined with its verse: "A liar's song is designed to tear truth into shreds." Each door added an unrecognized verse, such as, "Be He male, he'd be Satan from hell, be it the other…the angel of Death," but the song's ending was very clear: "Make me your murder and I will kill you all."

The last sentence scared me! Somehow the dream informed that they were real, live pirates. I looked around. I had lost my dreamself and I couldn't return the same way that I had entered. Quickly, I started looking for an exit by turning to the right.

The white doors on the left wall disappeared, as I turned to face a large archway. I was wondering where I was, when the dream called the place: "the chemotherapy cabinet."

The room identified the white cabinets as: A medical covenant built by a group of people who have made a pact to withhold medicines in order to build a medical job security bank by closing the door to common-sense drug usage in relationship to humanistic healthcare values. A place where medical customers were not allowed to enter or to know truthful medicine history.

I stood facing a large dark archway. There was no "exit" sign. Large 3-foot feathers, symbolizing a heavenly-gift/prize/treasure, hung across the top and halfway down each side.

The feathers represented themselves as medical gifts. The feathers also identified that they didn't belong to the person who had hung them. Each father was once a heavenly gift that fell to earth as a prize, a gift, and a golden treasure. The thief's gift was presented as a plague. Since each feather was identified as a separate item, I looked each feather over for an understandable meaning. The feather's original meaning and content had been rearranged. It appeared as garble. Only the person upon whom the prize was bestowed knew the original feather meaning. The feathers couldn't speak; yet, it was as if the feathers themselves were stating that the original owner or meaning was nowhere around, and that they were deliberately placed out of reach with their original medical design hidden.

I stepped back to take a quick count. There were between twenty and twenty-five feathers, and each one had been neatly nailed in place around the archway.

Again, I watched myself examining each feather over and over while saying, "One feather is Adriamycin." I even began to examine the feathers wondering if I was looking for a pill.

The feather at the archway center was the most eye-catching. It had far more layers of dust and cobwebs than any of the others. The reds and yellows showed the discoloration of considerable age. The shades of blues and greens remained slightly lustrous. The center feather itself gave me the impression that it had been hanging in the Humanity-in-Reverse-Cupboard for an extremely long time.

Again, I stepped back from the feathers. There was a problem with the cupboard's language. Then the dream again called the uninterpretable garbled words: "Humanity-in-Reverse-Cupboard."

The only thing I could clearly see was dust, feather size, and feather luster. The newly added last feather on the left side of the archway had an eye-catching rainbow metallic hue. I stared at all the feathers, saying, "No, I'm not leaving until I find it. It's here! I know it is. To come this far and not thoroughly examine each item would be foolishness."

I began looking again and carefully examining each feather. I could feel by the aura that the one item for which I was searching was there among the many feathers. I was totally baffled as to why I could not recognize it.

Then all of a sudden, the dream began to speak in a narrative voice: "First, I want you to meet the person who hung the feather for which you look."

A distinguished-looking man dressed in a gray business suit walked into the center of the dream through the feathered dark archway. He was carrying a 2'x1' white sign, with the numbers "1974."

The feathers had been moved and strung across the cupboard-room like a banner. The dark-haired man walked from the center to the right and stepped to a feather that was hanging three or four feathers to the right of the center. There at the feather he hung his 1974 sign. The unique business-looking gentleman then turned to face me, as the dream introduced his name and continued to narrate: "When you steal from God, do not think it goes unnoticed."

A second man came walking in. He, too, was carrying a 2'x1' white sign. I didn't see any lettering. The sign appeared blank.

A third person, a shorter, dark-haired woman followed quickly behind. She, too, carried a 2'x1' white sign with no visual print. I saw the right side of her soft, sweet facial features and her mid-length dark, flowing hair as she walked pass, and continued to walk to a second archway on the extreme right that lead back into the bright hospital corridor.

The second and third person had entered the dream quickly and were exiting when a fourth figure entered the dream holding a 2'x1' sign reading "1994." The faceless figure entered moving to the left, and stood in the shadows. It represented the newest hung feather.

I could feel myself thinking aloud and wondering, "Who are these people?"

I turned my head back to the right to see that the second man and the woman did not stop to claim a feather, they exited the dream through the bright archway that lead back into the hospital corridor. The narrator said each name and told of a special place where these people were kept, saying, "They will be called upon when the truth is searched."

I did not see the place to which the two walked. Once they passed through the hospital corridor archway, both disappeared. My attention then focused at the left and on the 1994 sign. I was in awe at the fourth profile standing by the most recent and brightly rainbow-colored bottom feather. It was as if that bright feather itself cast metallic hues, deliberately letting me know that it was the newest addition: "The best of the penicillin for the largest of the blood groups is now Humanity in Reverse."

I stared at the silhouette. It was like a self-image of me; the last of the blood groups was my own.

The narrator continued: "The humanity cupboard is now empty. The book is in its entirety and ready to be written backwards. Stealing from God is like stealing from your neighbor. The thieves should be handled like any other thief. The crime should appear in print. The items they stole and who they stole them from."

A nine-foot god-like figure moved, re-appearing under the feathered banner that was strung from the dark archway to the brightly-lit one. It was a recognizable image. The one that appeared on the cloth called the Shroud-of-Turin. The eyes on the God-like figure were closed.

The figure was the dream's narrator, saying: "What is my World War 2 doing here?"

The word "2" had an echo: II, two, to, and too. When the narrator spoke, it was more than a pun. The words spanned from earth to eternity.

The dream itself cast an aura, as if it, too, could speak, identifying the narrator: "When this figure walks, the ground will tremble."

The scene became like a large computer room, lighting up each circuit until the final function flashed "Glow" and the complete room lit every corner of the "how" and "why" the chemotherapy covenant had come into existence and that the covenant itself was the "Doom's Day Message."

The dream spanned to beyond my recognition. The only thing understandable was condensed to one sentence: "after death there will be no readers".

End of Dream

Instant Insanity
Chapter 23
August 9, 1996

A month had passed since Carl's common-bacterial-produced heart disease that required a cadaver to replace the bacterial-damaged area. The visiting nurse arrived for her scheduled visit. The patient who was my husband, and I had noticed a red spot that had the appearance of an infection. The visiting nurse, too, noticed that an infection was appearing in the area of the month-old pacemaker surgery. The nurse called the heart clinic.

Immediately, I drove my husband to the hospital for the heart specialist to look at the pacemaker-area infection. While Carl and I were in the waiting room, I shared the 10-page Doxorubicin antibiotic write-up found in the TOXNET hazardous substance bank with one of the heart office ladies. The dream titled "God Visits" was now two years old. It took me a long time to find the antibiotic that was a tumor fighter and also a virus fighter that was under the TOXNET N.L.M.'s Toxicology Data Network Hazardous Substance Data Bank. At the time of the first bombing of the World Trade Center, it was known that the drug-of-choice Gentamicin sulfate USP used on a six-week protocol would drug over-dose after a couple of weeks. Why not use several antibiotics, including one that was known to be antitumor/antiviral?

The heart clinic nurse made a copy of the interesting Doxorubicin antibiotic. It was made from a mutated bacterium discovered during the antibiotic era (1940-1960). We both thought that it was rather strange that there haven't been more antibiotics made from the mutated bacterium strands. That would be a part of cell/germ evolution.

A room was ready for Carl. Once inside Carl's hospital room, a Cardiologist entered (I call a cardiologist a heart specialist). The cardiologist called in an Internal Medicine doctor (I call an Internal Medicine doctor a drug specialist) for additional advice about the medication suggestions. Both specialists entered the room to join Carl and I. The Internal Medicine who wore the white drug specialist jacket also had what appeared as Carl's patient's folder (which should have contained his Gentamicin Sulfate USP drug over-dosing) in her hand. The drug specialist professional said, "Gentamicin Sulfate."

To my left a cool breeze had entered the room. The breeze represented the Hospital Ghost, whispering a Gentamicin Sulfate USP reminder. The air current intermixed with the drug specialist's freshly spoken words to bring attention to what was being said. Apparently the patient's folder held no information about the previous months sulfate drug overdose, nor did it contain the 10-page information on the patient's most effective antibiotic, Doxorubicin. So I said, "The Gentamicin Sulfate caused serious side-effects. It shut down Carls kidneys as much as the infection did!"

The drug specialist's head dropped as her facial expression snarled: <u>I am taught to be the Son of Satan. You have the nerve to question ME!</u>

It was as if she knew that the United States drug law removed all patients' rights to the more effective antibiotics. Calmly, the drug prescriber lifted a pleasant face, as a soft smile said, "We'll try Flagyl."

"That one caused diarrhea," I blurted. Then I remember that the diarrhea was in June, the month prior to Carl's heart surgery. Flagyl was discontinued after a very short amount of time, but it was used again at the hospital in July, so I asked, "When Carl was here last month, Flagyl was one of several antibiotics used. Carl had a drug reaction. There was a rash on both feet. Nothing was ever said about which antibiotic caused the rash -- a common visual-aid used for a drug/antibiotic reaction."

The expert drug prescriber was holding what appeared as Carl's medical folder, and yet, was prescribing every antibiotic that created additional problems! A medical customer should be informed about such reactions. The medical customer should have a copy of all his medical treatments and know what drugs he or she can or cannot take. After combining the questions about Carl's disappeared medical records that contained both the infection and antibiotic dilemmas, I wanted to know more about the second antibiotic choice by saying, "Besides Flagyl is made from E. Coli. One of the oldest known tumor producers."

The drug prescriber gave a sigh as if to say <u>this is my third and final choice. I will have to get a politician to pass a law where NO one questions a drug prescriber!</u> An unknown to me antibiotic was mentioned. Both doctors reassured Carl and I that it was a good one, and it was going to be the one used. A good antibiotic would show results in one day. It didn't. (Five days later on August 13, 1996, the drug specialist commented that the antibiotic didn't look like it was working. Be patient.)

Meanwhile, Carl wished to meet some of the hospital staff from his previous visit. It had been 18 days since he was released on July 22, 1996 after his heart surgery. Carl had arrived at the hospital by ambulance. Hence he didn't know that he had changed hospitals, so he never got to see much of this one.

Carl remembered many of his hallucinations from his previous visit, and he wanted the hospital staff to notice that his conversation and actions had greatly improved once he was removed from the drug influence.

The August hospitalization generated an additional $25,000 in hospital expenses. Personally, I would rather have the more effective antibiotics available to me.

Instant Insanity

Chapter 24

The Propaganda Carnival

The Propaganda Carnival dream had occurred the year after Carl's bacterial-infection produced heart disease, which required a cadaver body part to replaced the bacterial damage. Prior to Carl's bacterial-produced heart disease, he had two cancers that also had the appearance of untreated and improperly treated bacterial infections. I called the medical lies "Health Sabotage". I certainly wished that someone had told me about the century old evil doctor's curse. Corruption worked like skin cancer. First the cell-type personal infection appeared, then the sore-type deterioration spread. After the deterioration-spread, the point-of-origin would be ignored and deliberately lied about. Shortly after the Propaganda Carnival dream, I joined a national cancer study program. The study had shown that I had several health problems. By this time, I had established my personal blood test figures and I had a very good idea about what my more effective medicines would be. I had to pay an additional $90 in order to view my personalize blood test profile and the doctor would not prescribe my more effective medicines. After my cancer study episode, I would compare permitted bacterial infections with the permitted tuberculosis bacterial infections.

The Propaganda Carnival dream was the following:

In the twilight of my dream, I was on horseback, taking a mountain tour.

The slopes were filled with trees and a path was already there. Death was

my guide. When the four of us (guide, horse, donkey, and me) reached the

ledge at the mountain's peak, I jumped from the tour and dashed to solid

ground. I could hear my dreamself say: "You can go on without me." Before

the words all left my mouth, the ledge rock split in two. Half the rock,

the guide, the black horse and the donkey all plunged out of sight, dropping

to the Earth below.

I looked across the back-side-of-the-mountain. There was nothing there but

tree filled slopes with no civilization areas in sight.

Quickly, I remembered that there was civilization on the mountainside from

which we had climbed. I hiked down to the plateau.

The carnival had a Ferris wheel and many tents with sideshows. As I

approached, I could hear the merry-go-round's music and the churning of

machinery that worked the mechanical devices. Each sideshow was under

a tent and advertised with a flashing neon sign: Propaganda Heaven,

Passports, Hippocrates Hospital, and each tent had

a barker who stood like a mannequin at the entrance.

I walked up to the advertised hospital sign and spoke to the barker who

waved his arms and pointed his thumbs for people to enter. "Excuse me sir.

My guide, his horse, and a donkey just fell off a rock and plunged at least

a mile's drop to Earth."

"I'm doing my job. Leave them for the carnivores and the microbes. The

animals and the parasites have to eat too, you known."

I stepped inside the tent. Chairs were lined in several rows facing the

speaker on a platform. The chair on the end was empty. So I sat next to a

young lady clothed in a white nursing dress. "There's been an accident."

"I'm doing my job. Leave them for the carnivores and the microbes. The

animals and the parasites have to eat too. Hu-s-s-h. The speaker is about

to lecture."

"I am Hippocrates (460? -380? B.C.). I lived during an era when sickness

was believed to be caused by evil powers. It has now been proven that

illness is caused by evil powers. Yes. The demons will cause one kind of

sickness and the black magic produces another. Let us pray to the gods.

Yes. Pray to every one of the gods. We all know that truth is never hidden

in the Heavens. A mere mortal can unravel the myths. Let us use the art of calling upon our ancestors to uncover the already discovered medicines."

The speaker paused, looking to the Heavens, and continued, "Through timely

patience and impeccable honesty let us make an oath to the gods that we will

instruct according to a strict covenant, with purity and holiness: should

the flow of false medical words ever be permitted, then all the gods will

forever punish the liars."

I commented to the nurse: "I take it that the speaker's job is to lecture."

"That's right," the lady replied, adding: "You would make a good student."

I changed the subject, asking: "If I were to look for someone whose job might be an accident, where would I go?"

"The Ferris wheel."

I left Hippocrates Hospital tent to look for the Ferris wheel. It was the tallest item in the carnival. A short fence surrounded the ride. I could see three distinguished-looking men each dressed in a business suit and standing inside the fence next to the Ferris wheel operator who kept pulling the ride's switch. As I approached the Ferris wheel, I noticed information signs hung along the fence. I began reading each sign identifying the historic stops that had built the ride.

Sign #1. One hundred years ago the #1 disease killer was tuberculosis. Somebody voted to use chemicals on the TB patients in place of spending time or money on medical research for a vaccine. The money was then spent on sanatoriums and chemical research.

Sign #2. When the French discovered a vaccine in 1908, it was discredited and boycotted. The boycotting of a TB vaccine gave the medical professionals job security.

Sign #3. Job security was discovered in the medical theater. The price was to be paid for in life and in human suffering. Therefore, the term job security was not allowed to be mentioned even though it existed and was founded in the medical theater.

Sign #4. During Harry Truman's presidency (1945-1953), a drug amendment was passed: "Federal law prohibits dispensing (drugs) without prescription." The amendment was passed after the Second World War, when propaganda filled the air. The drug law gave the medical community more job security by withholding effective antibiotics.

The three men were bickering. I overheard the subject. It was about a job opening at the tyrant's tent. The businessman dressed in a gray suit said, "I was using the business approach. My healthcare employees were forever grateful that they had a job in a jobless era. Of course I felt bad about the tuberculosis patients who were affected by the vaccine boycott, but it was a medical financial necessity. Job security is important in any profession, including medicine. Life is a terminal disease. Sickness is never-ending." The two men to whom he spoke remained silent.

The man then placed his right hand to his face and ran all four fingers through a well-groomed graybeard. His beard was grayer than the gray hairs that intermixed with the brown strands on his head. The gray-suited man then moved his hand and pointed a finger to the Ferris wheel operator who was pulling the switch. "It was he who did the switch, using chemical substances in place of the natural phenomenon. It's him and his philosophy to use human parasites to promote human ignorance."

I found the man's philosophical concern to be interesting, so I asked, "What is your name sir?"

"That's not a part of my job."

For a brief moment, I had forgotten why I came to the Ferris wheel. "Oh-h-h, my guide just fell off the cliff. I'm looking for some assistance."

The nameless man dressed in the gray suit replied, "I really feel bad, but leave him to the carnivores and the microbes. The animals and the parasites have to eat too, you know.

I turned to the man pulling the switch. "There's been an accident."

Again the man pulled the Ferris wheel's switch lever, while saying, "I do my job very well. Leave them for the carnivores and the parasites."

I left and walked to the tent with the neon light display flashing Propaganda Heaven. First I stopped to speak with the barker who stood waving his arms and pointing his thumps to the entrance. "What do you do with accident victims?"

"Leave them for the carnivores and the microbes. The animals and the
parasites have to eat too, you know."

I entered the Propaganda Heaven tent. There were two oval tables. At the first table sat Adolph Hitler (1889-1945) and Joseph Stalin (1879-1953). An empty chair separated the two men.

Hitler and Stalin were conversing and having a debate as to which one was the best of the tyrants.

"I have more recorded historic kills than you."

"My philosophy that 'Death solves all problems' will live forever."

As they spoke, each man stared at the third empty chair, which sat in the middle separating the two.

Nikita Khrushchev (1894-1971) sat at the second table by himself and in a boastful manner, said: "I am the king of propaganda."

I remembered Khrushchev. He was the Soviet Union's Prime Minister when I was in high school. Khrushchev was a short man and a tad heavy, but a jolly
pleasant-looking older person. His hairline was the same as my grandfathers: a little gray around the ears and bald on the top. Unlike my grandfather he didn't speak English. In life, Khrushchev's words had to be translated.

Quickly, I remembered that Nikita Khrushchev had made a statement charging
Stalin with fostering a "cult of the individual". Khrushchev accused Stalin as a person who proclaimed himself a god, which was something that most dictators did. Therefore I didn't think that that was much of an excuse for Stalin not to let Khrushchev sit at the same table.

Then Khrushchev spoke, "For every penny that a U.S. dog spends to uncover the truth, a dollar of the U.S. taxpayers money is spent to discredit the effort."

Immediately, I had expected to hear "Leave them for the carnivores and the microbes!" So I questioned, "Are you talking to me?"

My words jolted me awake!

I immediately woke from the dream, wondering: "What did Khrushchev know about the 50's United States drug law 'CAUTION: Federal law prohibits the dispensing without prescription', that the people didn't? The law was passed during the Cold War Era. I believe that the law created a lying prescription drug god that used the prescription drug law to destroy the

United States antibiotic and vaccine policies.

Shortly after the dream, I saw a newspaper advertisement where the National Cancer Institute was looking for volunteers. I joined because both my husband and I were under the care of an evildoer doctor that would not give the better medicines to patients.

PLCO

Chapter 25

1998 &

March 12, 2001

What is the PLCO? In 1997, I saw a cancer institute advertisement Prostate, Lung, Colorectal, & Ovarian (PLCO) Cancer Screening Trial program. They were looking for volunteers. I decided to join. Prior to seeing the ad, I had a dream that I titled "Propaganda Carnival" where Nikita Khrushchev spoke: "For every penny that a U.S. dog spends to uncover the truth, a dollar of the U.S. taxpayers money is spent to discredit the effort."

I remembered Khrushchev's famous 1959 prediction that the United States would destroy itself from within. Since I, too, am being deprived of my more effective medicines, I immediately came to the conclusion that Khrushchev knew more about the United States drug law "CAUTION: Federal law prohibits dispensing without prescription" legalizing Health Sabotage than the people did. How does a study program affect the drug law? I joined the cancer study program to find out!

Treason used to be every Americans concern. In 1983, I considered Health Sabotage as a form of Treason. So in 1997, I joined the National Cancer testing study to see how taxpayer money was spent, and what happened during a test study.

My 1998 cancer screening test results discovered several health problems. The chest x-ray showed a spot on my lung, the CA125 blood test was 9.0, the ovarian ultrasound test results showed wall thickening and it was recommended that I see a doctor to have a biopsy done. Immediately in 1998, I spent $90 to go to a doctor for a better understanding of the health problems that the cancer study program had discovered. The doctor discovered a few more health problems in addition to what the cancer study did. I also had my blood re-drawn for a better understanding of the Blood Test called the "White Blood Cell Differential" in relationship with the CA125 blood test figure of 9 units/ml.

My 1998 "White Blood Cell Differential" appeared as the following:

Test Name	Results	Units	Range (Was)		Mine	
WBC	8.4	3.9-11.4	6			
Neutrophils	50.1	%	38-80	(54-62)	59	
Lymphocytes	36.2	%	15-50	(25-33)	30	
Monocytes	5.5	%	0-13	((3-7)	5	
Eosinophils	5.6	%	0-8	(0-3)	1	
Basophils	2.6	H	%	0-2	(0.05)	0.2

There were also additional interesting cell abnormalities.

Cholesterol/				
HDL Ratio	6.0	H	Ratio	3.7-5.6
Basophils	2.6	H	%	0-2
BASO ABS	0.22	H	T/CUMM	

My concern for my health was that bacteria that consumed cholesterol were going unnoticed and untreated. I believed that the United States President and his congress originally passed the prescription drug law to keep the 1908 BCG tuberculosis vaccine from ever being used in the United States. The United States medical advisors should have told the people how important blood tests were.

Untreated bacterial infections caused more than cancer. The bacteria will settle around the heart to produce heart disease.

It was my understanding that the "Steven ML. Fundamentals of Clinical Hematology, 1997" used the Basophils Range as 0-0.5%. Therefore when I asked about my Basophils being flagged as HIGH, I was told that it was only .6 high nothing to worry about and no antibiotics were needed. The lab had used a range figure that was four times higher. If the lab used a .5 figure and not the 2 figure, my abnormal cell count would have been 2.1 higher than what it should have been. To me that meant that I have to leave the States in order to purchase antibiotics for a simple bacterial infection.

Well, after Carl's 1983 biopsies, I've concluded that biopsies were for tissue only. The Bible called a liar "A Liar", and gave the reference "For the life of the flesh is in the blood. A Medical Liar would say, "Blood means nothing!" and a tissue biopsy would be "Suck the blood from the flesh". In 1983 every doctor/drug prescriber knew that antitumor antibiotics were being withheld in order to create a larger medical business. Blood problems were being omitted, which to me produced an inaccurate biopsy.

Prior to my March 2001 Prostrate, Lung, Colorectal and Ovarian Cancer Screening Trial, my husband had a hernia surgery in August 1999.

My cancer screening appointment was on March 12, 2001 at 10:30 a.m. Prior to my appointment, I had written a letter to the National Cancer address inquiring the location of Animal Air-Injection Studies. My appointment was south of my traveling bubble. I had to travel over 20 miles in a heavy traffic area and I seem to get lost whenever I travel on the roads south. So I gave myself an hour of getting-lost-time, which I did, but I arrived at the clinic a half-hour early. I had brought some reading material with me. I was re-reading "Blood Group – Antigens and Disease" a small 6"x9" burgundy colored book put out by the American Association of Blood Banks in 1983. I was again looking for the origination of an antibody test called the Blood Type Identification. The 1983 hematologist used the Blood Type Identification test to identify antigens that appeared in Carl's blood from the Coombs, Duffy and Kidd system for blood transfusions that were used in place of antitumor antibiotics to treat his 1983 neck tumor.

The first of three times that Carl cheated Death (or the Lying Devil Doctor) was in 1983. Carl had gone to a hematologist. The hematologist used blood transfusions instead of antitumor antibiotics to treat Carl's neck tumor.

A blood test called Blood Type Identification was done. So whenever I hear the words that the doctors did NOT check the blood prior to transfusion, I consider the statement a medical lie. Hematologists and other blood specialists were checking the blood!

By my appointment time, I had to use the rest room. When returned my name had been called, so I had to sign the patient-waiting list again. My name was called again after 11.

My first instruction was to go into the bathroom and empty my kidneys. Then I was led to an examining room. My lady guide then told me to strip from the waist down and put the hospital garment on with the tie in back. So I took off my black boots (I had dressed with the idea that the rain was going to change into snow), then my navy slacks, and underwear. I then put the hospital garment over my "Fighting Irish" sweatshirt and sat on the gurney. I kept staring at the blood vial box and thinking, "How is the bloodsucker going to draw my blood with this heavy navy sweatshirt on?"

I answered myself, "You dummy, you didn't hear the lady guide right! She must have said to take off all clothes!" I took off my heavy navy sweatshirt and opened the locked door, so that someone would know that I was sitting in the examining room waiting.

The first person to enter was the bloodsucker. Five blood tubes were drawn for the program test. "That's a lot of blood for only one blood test," I commented.

The bloodsucker replied, "The blood is tested for several things in addition to the CA-125 cancer blood test."

"Really," I replied, as I remembered my 1998 PLCO blood test. After my 1998 PLCO, I had many health problems. I visited a doctor, who then found more health problems in addition to what the PLCO cancer screen tests discovered. When I was at the doctor's, I also had my blood re-drawn in order to receive the blood test results. Once the blood tests were in my possession, I could read them myself! In 1983, I felt that lying about medical records was a form of Health Sabotage. The hematologist that Carl had gone to in 1983 actually had the capabilities of raising the blood test laboratory figures to an extra high figure where abnormal cells would not be flagged, therefore go unnoticed!

The blood draw inflicted pain, so I quickly decided to change the subject by saying, "I don't think that I'll join the Alcoholic Study. I deserve to be one, but it requires a blood test." Finally my five blood tubes were filled, and the bloodsucker removed the needle and her job was done.

The Ovarian test was next. A fairly young gal came in with the Ovarian- testing machine. I signed with the pleasant thought that if I'm going to babble about why I think that President Clinton should have been impeached in 1993 for giving a US enemy the right to dictate the US antibiotic drug policy, and every medical person would call patriotism assisting the enemy with medical lies, I should make sure that a painless test is being inflicted upon me!

"Antibiotics are being over-used," the young lady technician said, sounding like a pre-recorded message.

"What about the under-used antibiotics?" I had my doctor's referral with my copy of the few PLCO tests results in my purse. I was going to a doctor that discouraged antibiotic use. When I asked for antibiotics to treat my many health problems, the doctor gave me a referral to go to another doctor some where in Southfield (which is way out of my bubble). I used my hand to I hit myself in the head to get back on the under-used antibiotic subject. " doctors have been lying to their patients since the 1908 tuberculosis vaccine."

The clinic's employee relied, "I don't think that I've ever heard of a tuberculosis vaccine!"

"That's right, you probably haven't. Doctors did NOT want a tuberculosis vaccine discovered, and when one was, they didn't want it used!" I was getting into the subject about withheld-under-used antitumor antibiotics, when that portion of the PLCO test was over.

The next PLCO test was the check x-ray. In 1998, a spot on my lung was detected. There were two other ladies waiting for the chest x-ray. Again, I took off my clothes, and put the hospital gown on, and sat with the two black ladies to chat. My name was called first. I had the chest x-ray, got dressed, and returned home.

When I received the March 2001 report, all health problems had disappeared, even though the cancer cell count had increased.

Instant Insanity
Chapter 26

PLCO—October 22, 2001

After my March 12, 2001, the next PLCO appointment was to be on October 22, 2001. The evening after the March 12, 2001 PLCO appointment, I had a dream that explained how the lying serpent crawled into my life. The dream was extremely lengthy, but when I woke to write it down my words became lost in a jumble of thoughts. The dream covered four different subjects. Soon the thoughts went Poof and my words were scribbled as "Duh".

The dream had informed that it was known in 1977 that infections that seeped into the blood from the gums would cause cancers. What a shock my husband's 1996 bacterial-produced heart disease was! I had noticed that when I had a tooth infection, it produced cell abnormalities. I had also noticed that doctors do not prescribe antibiotics, even when the cell abnormalities were flagged.

Reality was that I didn't look at my right arm where the blood was drawn. The following day, I did look at my right arm. The blood draw had left it with bruises.

When I received the brief copy of my March 2001 PLCO test, all health problems had disappeared, but the CA125 blood test showed an elevation. The CA125 blood test was supposed to detect cancer. A study would identify the CA125 relationship with the white and red blood cells. Any idiot would know that looking at one test would be like viewing the blood with one blind eye and the other eye closed.

Meanwhile, the blood-draw bruises continued to become larger. My first thought was that too much air could have been injected when the vacuum was created to draw the blood. I then thought, "Where can I go to find out about the animal air injection studies?"

That night in a dream, once again I could see the Death Rider as he moved from the left distant dark horizon to the right, shouting, "You lost the cold war!"

I turned my head and stretched my neck to strain my eyes in the direction of the voice in order to see where they shadowy figure disappeared. The Death Rider was nowhere in sight. End of dream.

Upon waking, I checked a few dictionaries. A phlebotomist must be a fairly new word. In my 1983 medical dictionary only the word "phlebotomus" (a bloodsucking sand fly) appeared.

Then I decided to enter Newsgroups, looking for information about air injections and bruises from a blood draw. The people on the Internet were fabulous. Indeed a great improvement from trying to make phone calls that answer with a recording, give you a run-around, and then hang up before any questions could be asked or answered.

The Internet Newsgroup people offered several replies. A person named "me" told me, "The larger needle is more likely to leave a bruise. The bigger hole in your vein equals a longer time to make a good seal, and the greater likelihood of seepage. I take offense at LK's statement that 'In any case, it's a frequent consequence of clumsy needle handling.' Hey, somebody has to stand up for us vampires."

One person gave a scary comment on air injection: "Air is only harmful, if injected in large quantities."

I had already heard that a patient had to request "No air please! Some people die, some people don't and God only knows what happens to those in the middle!"

After leaving my Internet friends, I returned to the dream world.

Dreams could be used as a tool to identify areas of simply understanding and even simple solutions. An example would be the following:

The dream gave the title "Eye of the Storm". I looked carefully at all the details. It was a bright, calm, clear day. The scene was filled with green rolling hills and scattered with people. The people were picking up their fallen debris that resulted from the passing storm. I, too, was like the rest of the dream people who were gathering reminisce. I could see myself moving and rummaging through the pile of rubble in front of my dream face. The people and debris were scattered, yet every one was chatting. Each voice was clear, as the person spoke.

I picked up a piece of wood, and said, "Yep, it reminds me of home."

There was a chuckle within the dream's atmosphere. The item I held was only debris, which was an example of the only thing, the storm had left behind. I woke with the feeling that it was more than debris. The rest of the storm had yet to be. End of dream.

"Wow," I thought, "what a simple dream. There must be a simple reality solution." My problem was to find a new doctor and pay big bucks to have my blood redraw. I didn't wish to pay extra money, again, just so that I could compare a larger picture with the CA125 blood tests. That would be the pit of stupidity. Therefore, I decided to request the complete blood tests from the cancer study.

The telephone rang. Instead of giving a written reply, the co-ordinator called. Well, the co-ordinator proceeded to tell me that the girl who drew my blood in March was misinformed about additional blood test. The study program drew five vials, but only tested for the one CA125 blood test. The rest of the blood was then deep-frozen in cryo vials to be studied in the future.

Previously, I had noticed that one very big problem of comparing a dream that involves health and healthcare was the medical records. An example of that was Dr. Garcia. So, I mentioned that it would be nice if she wrote it down.

The PLCO co-ordinator then snapped, "Maybe I should send you a copy of the consent form you signed!" A mental picture also appeared with her thoughts saying, "You Slut! You have the nerve to question a member of the Medical Liars Society!"

I replied, "Maybe you should cancer my October 22, 2001 PLCO appointment!"

The PLCO co-ordinator mailed me a copy of the consent form in place of her verbal reply. I felt that was an example of a Lying Serpent. Why? Only a serpent would call to tell a lie, and then not place the lie in print. The PLCO co-ordinator provoked a new question. What would it take for you to call Health Sabotage "Health Sabotage"?

Another no answer would be The End of my volunteering to be on this Cancer Study Program!

Instant Insanity

Chapter 27

Clear IV-line Air

August 29, 1999

The advantage of a dream log would be referring back to the original dream.

Several weeks prior to my husband's IV line containing 8-inches of solid air, I woke remembering a dream conversation. "Amazing that he died. It was a simple procedure. I find the death hard to believe."

The dream was blurred, and the name was muffled. I felt slightly sickly when I woke. I knew that some deaths were unavoidable, so I didn't go back into the dream to ask more questions.

Shortly thereafter I completely forgot about the dream until Thursday August 26, 1999 when my husband was scheduled as an outpatient for a 45-minute hernia surgery. The first antibiotic mentioned was Gentamicin Sulfate, which was the same antibiotic that he was drug over-dosed on in June 1996. Meanwhile in August 1999, a $90 bill was sent from Heart Clinic for the service of telling my husband to find a hernia surgeon. Normally the office call was $50. For three years the Heart Clinic specialists told Carl not to worry about the hernia. I thought that the $90 bill to tell someone to go someplace else for medical service was outrageous. So I wrote a $50 check and a letter asking if my husband's records contained the fact that he was Gentamicin sulfate USP drug over-dosed in June 1996!

Anyway, the 45-minute hernia surgery took three hours! The hernia surgery was in the same place where the two crossed band-aides had appeared in July 1996, where a test was done on the colon. An incision was made to check for kidney tissue, prior to the cadaver replacing the bacterial heart damage. The surgeon was shocked to see stepping-stone colon tissue. The unusual scar tissue had made sense to me. The body would be scared with every cut made upon it.

Carl's outpatient surgery turned into a five-day hospitalization. On Sunday August 29, 1999 Carl was still hospitalized when his IV machine began beeping. I looked at the machine. The computer was flashing the words "Clear Air."

Two nurses came into the room. One was young, while the other mature. The young nurse said that she didn't know anything about IV-machines. The mature nurse said, "Now's the time to learn", and she quickly left the room. The young nurse fiddled with the gadget. It was obvious that she was new and unfamiliar with the IV machine. She was having trouble operating the computer part of the IV machine. Since it said "Clear Air", I watched a little closer to see how that was done. The nurse opened the computer door to place 18-inches of IV line below the computer sensor in order to make the beeping stop, and she left the room.

I walked over to check. The line contained 8-inches of solid air. I tried snapping the line, but all I did was move the air around. Because of all the lies that Carl had heard, he was upset with me tampering with the IV line, and he said, "She knows what she's doing! Leave it alone!" As we argued, the air was moving slowly toward his arm, so I went and got the young nurse, which made Carl even more disgusted. The nurse looked at the line and grabbed a needled-suction thingy and removed the air bubbles, explaining that a few air bubbles didn't really matter.

The Air Bubbles reminded me about my June-11-96 Fox Clinic visit when I had mentioned the air bubbles and the Psycho-evaluator immediately thought that I could kill someone handling an IV line. I had always heard that an IV-line should contain NO AIR! At the time I had air bubbles, I didn't know how to remove them, and the IV-line was NOT hooked up to a person.

Within minutes, Carl's mother and sister entered the room to visit.

The young nurse returned while Carl's mother and sister were there. The nurse asked two questions in one sentence, which caused a slight confusion. The three of us (nurse, Carl and I) were still in an ugly mood about the 8-inches in the IV-line. Carl spoke snappy words. The nurse left the room. I, too, left the room to go have a cigarette. Life would be much easier, if I could find a doctor that would give a good antibiotic! The prescription drug law had also deprived me the right to my more effective medicines!

In the dream someone died because of a simple action either done or undone. In the case of withholding antitumor/antiviral antibiotics, as such this one was the young nurse would be doing the medical client a favor. After 2 decades of not receiving a prescription for his most effective antibiotics and having to go through the pain of having the bacterial infection surgically removed over and over, she would be putting a medical client out of his misery. (Drugs are federal. Why am I the only person noticing the withholding of antitumor/antiviral antibiotics?) The removing of effect antibiotics should affect everyone living in the United States.

At the time of the first World Trade Center bombing, every medical advisor knew that the drug-of-choice

Gentamicin Sulfate USP (a 2 would drug over-dose the patient halfway through the recommended 6-week protocol. The American Spirit was known as Organ Thieves. In 1996 every heart specialist at the Heart Clinic knew that my husband was drug over-dosed. They knew that Gentamicin was used for only two weeks.

The medical society made more money treating cancers and organ transplantations than prescribing antibiotics that might cure the medical client. At the time of the 2001 World Trade Center bombing, the official United States god was in two places, on the United States money and with the drug prescriber. The Bible called a liar "a liar". I called the prescription drug law "The lie for me, die for me god". I was under the impression that over-used antibiotics were because the drug prescriber would only prescribe a limited number of antibiotics.

I had also found it interesting that the Bible stated that the blood fed the flesh. Carl's hernia biopsy was interesting that it was only about the tissue. No blood specimen appeared anywhere. The scared tissue was called adhesions.

At the time of the air incident, it appeared as an error. One explanation was that the Henry Ford Hospital experts stated that it took 100cc of air to kill a dog. I believed that the information was probably also an error. Anyway, when

Carl's doctor was hospitalized, the doctor died while in the hospital. If the doctor died because of IV-air-injection, the fact would not be mentioned. I believed that the false information about air injection would prevail the same way that Gentamicin Sulfate drug over-dosing had.

Instant Insanity
Chapter 28
Watching Mother Die

We all know that death is a part of life. Dying to some people, myself included, has become as much a part of life as living. What I noticed most about mother's dreams were the acceptable death signs and that many medical truths were disappearing.

Mother began officially dying on the evening of November 8th, but she didn't stop breathing until November 10, 1999, during the last three days of her life she never completely slept. The dream people had become a significant part of human behavior and they were noticeable with mother. The scientific-studied suggested death rattle and old age clad-coloring death phenomenon was either disguised or not present in the way the scientific study had been deciphered. By this time it should have been common knowledge that physicians have been withholding antitumor antibiotics for decades.

One example would be the antibiotics Adriamycin and Bleomycin. They were my husband's most effective antibiotics and Bleomycin didn't disappear into the chemotherapy drug hazardous substance data bank cupboard until 1984. Back then medical people would tell my husband that Adriamycin and Bleomycin were not antibiotics. It created tremendous unnecessary family stress not to speak of the remorse of the loss of one's most effective antibiotics.

I made a list of what that one medical lie about antibiotics promoted:

1) Turmoil past, present and future: since the antibiotic Adriamycin was removed from the general medical list of common antibiotics back in 1974, and no NEW antibiotics were made from mutated bacterium. 2) Agitation: Family disaster, 3) Bickering: Family vengeance, 4) Clamor: Family rivalry stating that medical people do not lie, when in reality they did. 5) Commotion: Crimes of love...killing your spouse, as an act of mercy. 6) Confused: Emotional revolt, 7) Discord: Conflict with all gods, except the god of lies, 8) Disorderly: Erroneous judgment, 9) Disturbance: Sickly and fatal, 10) Hassle: Obstacles to normal everyday living, 11) Tumult: Crimes of vengeance seeking, and 12) Uproar: Mad and Madness for the destruction of your country.

First I should give information about mother's dying. Mother had two choices: a chest biopsy (Carl's pathogen infection was known to produce a tumor most commonly found in the neck, check, and groin), or no treatment at all.

She never had an antibiotic choice; therefore mother had been in pain from January to her death in November 1999. On October 7, 1999, mother's doctor recommended that she receive the recommended flu shot, and her health quickly failed daily. I felt that the adding of a new virus to an already germ filled body was NOT going to be for the better. Finally the week after mother's flu shot, she was in so much pain that she agreed to a biopsy to be done on her swollen and painful right arm. Mother's malignant diagnosed arm biopsy was called an inflammation with no infection.

Younger brother Elijah and I were doing what I called "The death guard watch," while young Elijah called it "Musical Chairs." Young brother's version was who was going to be the person left standing when the music stopped and mother died?

Mother and I would talk about the subjects in her dreams. Dreams often tell about death. The dream people would lurk in the shadows. Mother and I both had noticed that her drugs, especially because she was on morphine sulfate USP and her dreams would merge with reality.

Meanwhile, older brother Mike, the table-maker for the 1978 Shroud of Turin scientific test, flew in from out-of-state. He was under the impression that the withholding of effective antibiotics only took place here. Mike was surprised that people here had no legal medical rights when it came to receiving their most known effective treatments or antibiotics. Father and I tried to explain that the medical society was able to have lawmakers legalize the right to medically lies in every way possible.

So Mike thought it best that he sleep in mother's room in order to hear her every move. By this time the withholding of Mother's effective antibiotics had permitted the pathogens, the septic bacteria, and all those known parasite microorganisms to move in and take its toll.

People used to take photos of their loved one while watching what was known as The Great Death. I took a photo of Mike combing mother's hair. Mike posed for it, and afterwards he changed his mind.

During the evening of November 8th I thought that the time was 1:30 a.m., when mother's breathing took a turn for the worst. It was as if the dream people were there at mother's side and working like germ parasite mimics. Germ parasites couldn't have a hammer and chisel; the phrase "The dream people used a chisel to hammer holes into mother's heart and lungs" would be simply a metaphor about bacteria destruction. Mike thought that it was midnight.

Immediately brother and I argued over the time. I looked at the clock and it was 1:30 when older brother called young Elijah to come and join us.

Elijah and his wife came over to sit with older brother, dad and me to Watch Mother Die, but it turned out that we were watching mother gasping for air, thrashing, and sweating with beads of water on her forehead until daylight.

When the RN arrived, she explained that gasping for air was not painful. It looked painful, but it was like drowning. Drowning was not painful; it was simply uncomfortable. To me and because so many tumors and cancers used to be germ parasite produced, mother's situation looked more like septic bacteria had moved in and the germ parasites were destroying her heart valve, so I didn't invite my husband. The family continued to watch mother drown, gasping for air and thrashing with her eyes rolling to the back of her head. Then the dream people, still working like germ parasites,

used their hands to beat upon mother's kidneys until the kidneys ruptured, causing blood to mix with the urine that was flowing into the plastic sack that was used as a visual aid to show that death was not far away. The medical verbiage contradicted what the dream people said, so I again asked: "Are you sure mother is not in pain."

"Nope. No pain, simply the drowning effect."

Meanwhile dad was also sick, but dad had been ill for many years with no exact disease-identified problem. Dad too had visited the doctor on October 7, 1999. He was given the label of mother's prime healthy caretaker and he received the pneumonia vaccination, since that day his health was also failing daily. Dad was acting like he may have had a mini-stroke and he also had a throat fungus infection, along with a half-a-dozen other ailments.

The Watching Mother Die stress became so intense that between 9 and 10 p.m., I thought that we were going to have a double-header death crisis. Dad was wandering around in dementia-land. I hated to interrupt Mike, who was on the telephone for an hour, but I did and Mike replied, "It's not my time to watch dad!"

I felt uncomfortable about waking Elijah who was sleeping in the basement. Fortunately Elijah woke and came upstairs to help with the double dilemma. Then we all calmed down and continued to watch mother die. Again we watched mother die until daylight.

On November 10, at 10:53 a.m. mother was given a sedative (1 mg Ativan) shot to relax her from thrashing and sweating, and we all thanked the wonderful medical god for this token of relief. Of course my feelings were that any State that gives a medical license to withhold effective antibiotics should give sedatives and painkillers Free to the people who are afflicted with these improper-unidentified inflammations. Again we continued to watch mother die until we were again disgustingly bored.

Between 4 and 5 p.m., I was outside having a cigarette when I saw a neighbor changing their garage light bulb. The parent's condo also had a garage light bulb burnt out, so I walked over to see how the light fixture came apart.

The friendly neighbor came over with her step stool and a light bulb to change the light for us. When I walked into the condo, dad was laying on the hallway floor face up. I asked, "Okay brothers, what is wrong with dad?"

It turned out to be nothing important. Young Elijah decided to go home for a while. Mike and Dad went into the kitchen. It must have been my turn to watch mother die. Did I explain that the time of death was needed for the death certificate?

I looked at the clock which stated 5:00 p.m., I felt tired. To me the way Mother was breathing, she looked like she was good for another day. So I made myself a bed inside the closet where I could see her when I opened my tired eyes to check on her now and then. I found myself dozing off and while I slept I heard a dream voice say, "Write watching mother die today, yesterday, and the day before."

At that moment, Brother Mike came into the room and caught me dozing. "How can you see her from inside the closet?"

I explained, "I have a clear view of mother's face and her heavy breathing. If she stops breathing, I will notice."

Brother sat down in a chair next to mother because he didn't like the way I was doing the deathwatch. So I got up and wandered downstairs to type the dream's suggestion.

At 7:00 p.m., I heard Mike walk out of the room and into the kitchen. There was no visible way that Mike could see mother from the kitchen. So I wandered upstairs to do the deathwatch, after all we were asked to write down the time of death. I sat down next to mother. I noticed that mother's forehead had small beads of sweat; something similar to when she was thrashing and had large beads of sweat. I wiped her forehead and checked to see if her skin felt clammy as it had when the sweat beads were larger then I sat back down to watch. Don't get me wrong with the idea that there is a good way to die. Nobody wants to die.

If you were going to die, the painless drowning theory would probably be true after you were knocked unconscious.

By this time I thought that I would go and get myself a glass of milk and a couple of snacks. I was gone for maybe a minute. As I entered the room, I noticed that mother was no longer breathing. I put my milk and snacks down.

Mother was no longer gasping. Then I touched mother's forehead. It wasn't clammy like it was when I had left the room. The time was 7:05. I thought mother was dead, so I went and called Mike into the room. Mike asked, "Did you check her pulse?"

"No. I figured she didn't have one."

"Well," Mike snapped, "she is not officially dead until you discover that she doesn't have a pulse. The time is 7:10."

I looked at the clock on mother's right. It said 7:08. Mike was looking at the clock on mother's left; it said 7:10.

Mike then picked up the telephone to call Elijah and tell him that mother officially died at 7:10. We waited for Elijah to arrive before we called the police.

The police didn't have mother's Do Not Resuscitate (DNR) request on file. Actually the medical abbreviations

DNR was a relatively new word added to the medical clients vocabulary. Therefore the police had to send the EMS first.

After the EMS verified that mother was dead, then a policeman arrived. When the policeman filled out the 911-call form, he asked who was present at the time of death.

I raised my arm chest high and waved my hand to the right, saying, "I got the musical chair. I was awestruck that I was actually standing when I noticed that mother wasn't breathing."

The policeman rephrased his sentence: "You were all present!"

Mike placed his finger to his lips, "Hush, Kristine. You open your mouth again and the policeman will think that there was foul play here!"

Elijah then begins assisting with the form, "This was an expected thing."

I thought that I would include this chapter, because of all the paperwork involved when someone chooses to die at home with family members present. Everyone involved certainly reacted differently.

Instant Insanity

Chapter 29

Re-live

The dream's breath called itself a "Re-live". The air within a dream could often tell what the dream contained, as was in this case. The dream was reminiscing the question "Where did the bacterial-produced heart disease come from?" The dreams tiny air particles reflected the daily activities with memories of the cadaver replacing the bacterial damage in 1996. My husband had received no antibiotics after his 1994 cancer surgery. Two years after the cancer surgery, Carl then had common bacterial-produced Endocarditis. The dream itself contained reminders of the 1996 surgery and what had happened during the 25 hospitalization days. It was a "Then and Now" comparison-type dream.

At the time of the 1993 World Trade Center bombing, the American Spirit was known as organ thieves. The drug-of-choice to treat bacterial-produced heart disease Endocarditis was a 6-week protocol of Gentamicin Sulfate USP, and it was known that halfway through the recommended protocol the patient would be drug over-dosed.

In 1996, the family couldn't understand Carl's cardiologist's words, "You make it thought this, it will be like hitting a home run."

Doctors have lied to the patient and public for a century. A century ago, the #1 highly contagious disease killer bacteria were known as the Tuberculosis family. doctors did NOT wish that a tuberculosis vaccine would be discovered and when one was, they cursed the discovery of the 1908 BCG tuberculosis vaccine and swore to Satan that it would never be used in the United States.

The evil doctors had to get a United States President and his congress to pass the prescription drug law "CAUTION: Federal law prohibits dispensing without prescription" to fulfill the evil curse. The evil curse then spanned into the United States antibiotic policies.

In the dream, I was again explaining to Cousin Webeyes that the BCG tuberculosis vaccine was never used in the United States. The person who said that it was had lied.

All of a sudden the lying Catholic nurse entered the scene. The tiny air particles reflected all of her previous lies. The lies were "Blood test mean NOTHING. The 1983 biopsy report was NOT a biopsy. The 1983 fourth-stage Hodgkin's disease was NOT fourth-stage Hodgkin's disease. Laboratory figures that are raised 10 times higher than normal mean nothing. Air injections are good. Antibiotics are bad."

I was in awe at the lying presence. The Catholic nurse was unclothed, standing there with her hands in back of her neck, shaking her tits and wiggling her butt, and saying, "I've had the tuberculosis vaccine."

I became annoyed with the liar, and asked, "Is there no end to your lies? Every lie you say supports Health Sabotage and its ungodly destruction."

The scene changed, reflecting back to the 1996 Gentamicin Sulfate USP over-dosing. The prayers that echoed though the hospital halls were "Someone please die for my organ installer. He and all his medical helpers need a job". It then became clear what the cardiologist was referring to.

The day before Halloween 2001, I was again at the hospital. It's a large complex with several medical buildings. The opposite side of the complex contained a 1913 mortar sign that housed the deceased spirits of souls that had died before their time. The old Tuberculosis (TB) treatment center spirits remained as a reminder that the tuberculosis bacteria had never disappeared. The tuberculosis bacteria were never eradicated, even though TB was replaced with Heart Disease as the #1 disease killer in the United States.

The doctors and nurses had to lie to keep the evil curse alive. More money was made treating the disease with chemicals and studying the disease and then studying the chemical treatments. The choice of the BCG tuberculosis vaccine was never given. Hence the phrase "The treatment is as deadly as the disease" became the popular evil doctor's medical philosophy.

Thereafter the evil doctors began to destroy the antibiotic policies. More money was made treating cancers and performing organ transplantations. The official prayer of the old and the new echoed the grounds. The prayer that was in 1913 "I'll see you dead before I see the 1908 tuberculosis vaccine used" was now "I'll see you dead before I use an effective antibiotic".

The re-live dream informed that when the bacteria reappeared, it would be with great vengeance. "Better start praying for an organ, now," the dream informed.

I was baffled. I had already tried praying for our most effective gram-negative antibiotics, but the prayers fell upon the drug prescribers' deaf ears. It was common knowledge that the drug-of-choice was what made the drug prescriber the most money.

The scene changed. I visualized what had appeared as an honest visiting nurse when she first arrived after my husband's 1996-heart surgery. In reality, the nurse had shown me her instruction sheet. The complete page was unclear straight lines (//////). The nurse had never seen an instruction sheet appear totally unclear. The nurse showed me the page, but then she wouldn't let me have a copy.

The re-live scene changed again. This time to when Carl had his 1996 pacemaker area infect. It was clear that medical students were taught to ignore bacterial infections and use only the drug-of-choice. Treating sick people was the job. Whether the patient lived in complete pain, sickness, or died was a trivial.

Instant Insanity

Chapter 30

Watching Father Die

On November 28, 2001, Dad fell while walking to or from the dining room. He was an 80-year-old who was living at an assisted-living complex. Dad's health had been failing. He had gone from 160 pounds to 105. When dad fell, he apparently broke his hip, and he was taken to the hospital. Dad had a nurse on the evening that he died. The nurse knew that two surgeries on an 80-year-old man who never had a prior surgery would die. The nurse was shocked that the doctor had not given a warning!

My 81-year-old mother-in-law, Maxine wished to know all of dad's death details. Maxine's husband Sherman had died while in the hospital because of complications that had developed from and during his hip surgery. Apparently, now in December 2001, Maxine's doctor had told her that she was in need of surgery, but at her age, the surgical pain might kill her. Maxine also had informed that she weighed 155 pounds and had not filed her Living Will.

The day after dad fell, a doctor called me. I knew dad's health had been failing. The fall seemed the beginning of the end, and I said: "Father is old and frail." The doctor's tone of voice seemed designed to put me on a guilt trip, as he said, "Are you going to leave this poor man in pain?"

When dad could speak for himself, he declined all surgeries; but when he made out his Living Will, he did not include "No Surgeries". Had dad included "No Surgeries", I would have replied to the doctor, "Yes. We'll make arrangements for hospice." Instead, I replied, "Call my brother…he's in charge of that."

Mother-in-law then asked, "Where were your dad's medical records? My doctor hands me all my medical records…I don't even have to ask for them."

Apparently, the doctor didn't have any of dad's medical records and he had to make his own. When the doctor discovered that dad had not had a surgery in 50 or more years, it was one surgery after another. Dad was hospitalized from November 28, 2001 to his painful death on December 12, 2001.

First it was a hip surgery, then an amputation to the knee. I was not aware of the amputation. The day after, I visited dad. He had been in constant pain since he had entered the hospital. So, when I saw dad sleeping, I began chatting with the people visiting the patient in the next bed.

A doctor entered the room to see dad. I asked about the possible gangrene that my brother mentioned. The doctor removed the sheets to look at dad's foot. I didn't see dad's foot. I asked, "Where's his foot?"

The doctor replied, "Foot?"

Since I don't speak clearly, I have to say something several times. "Yes, foot," and I pointed to my feet, saying, "I have two feet, you have two feet...dad had two feet... those things at the bottom of your legs."

The doctor moved from the foot of the bed to the center, saying, "Let's see," and he pulled the sheets from dad's body.

My first thought was that his foot was tucked under his body. Then the light bulb clicked, "Oh my God, it's been amputated!"

The doctor motioned with his fingers, as if to say, "Come with me retard." I followed him into the hall where he pointed to father's room and said, "What for you do that?"

Immediately, I knew that he was referring to the amputation. Any retard could tell that both surgeries were an example of Human Exploitation. If there were gangrene, it would have showed up with the first blood test. It was like a game of charades where we talked with our hands and could understand each other perfectly. "Well," I said, "I have an 81-year-old mother-in-law," I turned pointing to Room 555, "who would like to know all the details about that."

We both knew that I was talking about father's amputation.

"I understand," the doctor said, while placing his hands behind his butt, and continuing, "I am only talking to myself. If that were my father, he would have died at home with some kind of dignity. Huhhhhh, nothing like that." And he waved his left hand toward the room with a disgust expression. Then the kind doctor gave several good suggestions.

I returned home and e-mailed Brother who replied, "When a doctor tells you to amputate to remove the gangrene…He is the doctor, so you agree to amputate! Who did you talk to the Hospital Janitor?"

The next day, my husband and I visited dad. He was lying on his side, appearing to be asleep with his eyes half open. Dad's food came about 5 p.m. The man in the next bed told me that dad had eaten in the morning, but they had had to feed him.

It was difficult to feed dad while he was lying on his side. So, when they came to pick up his tray, I asked if sitting up would help dad eat better.

Two people entered the room to move the 80-pound-man to a sitting up position. Dad's eyes popped wide open. His eyes seemed to be screaming with as much pain as his voice was. I couldn't believe the pain Dad was in, as he screamed: "God damn what are you doing to me now". Immediately, I wished that I had not asked dad to be moved to a sitting position. The two people who moved Dad explained that his butt sores were what was giving him pain. I was shocked at the words "butt-sores". Dad didn't have butt-sores when I was told to tell dad to poop in his pants the week prior.

I tried to feed dad some vanilla ice cream. His breathing was heavy and rattled. Dad's last meal was three small spoons of vanilla ice cream…the ice cream actually had to melt and run down his throat. Then he didn't want any more. I quit the feeding and sat down.

Dad's nurse came into the room. Most people know about the 1908 tuberculosis vaccine that was never used here. So, I started chatting with dad's nurse to see if she knew about the vaccine. Had the vaccine not been withheld, it would have been developed into a much better one. The man in the next bed joined in our conversation. As we chatted, the nurse turned her head to look at dad. His head was laid back on the pillow, his eyes half open and his mouth was fully opened. I thought I saw his chest move; it was probably his last breath.

The nurse placed her stethoscope on dad's chest, shaking her head. At 6:30, a doctor entered the room and officially declared dad dead. I considered myself blessed that I was present when both of my parents had passed on. In Dad's case it was obvious that he died of surgical pain, and I wondered if the doctor who declared dad officially dead would be calling the cause-of-death: surgical pain? My husband offered his suggestion. The doctor probably said to cut off the limb and replace it with plastic. Hummm, that was an interesting observation. The needed amputation would be whether or not dad was being fitted for a new limb. Why remove a limb, and leave a person bedridden to die to the poop-filled bacterial parasites?

The next day, dad was to go to a convalescent home to die of old age because he needed special care for his frail condition. So, why mention "Watching Father Die" and how he died without dignity weighing 80 pounds?

Again, I mention that my 81-year-old mother-in-law wished to know every detail. On the day my father died, Maxine weighted the same as she did 10 years ago. Maxine's an independent elderly person who couldn't understand why dad's medical records were NOT available to all of dad's doctors at the hospital. (I'm still working on the list of her questions.)

Apparently, Dad did not go to a lawyer to file his right-to-die with dignity. He did not state where he wished to die: at home with family or in a convalescent home around strangers. Dad also did not state that when he could not speak for himself, he did not wish that his body parts be removed, which he felt would leave him totally, painfully bedridden until death. The message to the United States elderly would be go to an attorney and put it in writing: "Please don't kill me with surgical pain."

It used to be that you paid your doctor to save your life. This was a clear case of paying a doctor to painfully kill you.

Meanwhile, I had been complaining how the Prescription Drug Law removed my right to my more effective antibiotics. The people who know me know that I would be saying, "Back in 1908 when the patriots were singing "God bless America," the evil doctors were praying to Satan, saying: "I'll see you and your siblings sick and dead before I see you receive a tuberculosis vaccine."

All of a sudden an unknown voice, said: "Go to the hospital pharmacy to purchase streptomycin in an ointment form; or in any available form."

Immediately, I could visualize the hospital pharmacist, saying: "I would see country (United Stated), truth and you dead before I sell you the antibiotic streptomycin without a prescription!"

Since I'm mentally slow and easily sidetracked, returning to the hospital pharmacy to purchase Streptomycin remained on my list of things to do.

Instant Insanity

Chapter 31

Hiring A Hit Man

In my dream log dated December 4, 2001, I had woke remembering that I had again had met with a trio-of-liars. Past experience had shown that it was filled with them and the only way a liar could be proved would be to confront the lie.

I had a red Jamaican Voodoo doll hanging above my computer to protect it from all viruses. I decided to place the doll in my left pocket, after which I drove to Livonia to visit Dad.

When I arrived, Dad was awake. He was trying to use the bar overhead to move his position. It was painful for him to slightly move. Then Dad said that he had to poop. I walked to the nurse's station to say that dad had to poop (bedpans used to be used). The lady told me that dad had pants on, so he could poop in his pants. I reminded me of the reverse of when you prayed to all the gods that your child would leave diapers to use the toilet. I returned to Dad to tell him that he could poop in his pants.

Dad scowled, so I sang the Poop Song, "I've got-t-a poop. You've got-t-a poop. We've all got-t-a poop. So poop, poop, poop, and you'll feel better."

A half-hour prior to Dad's death, the subject about his butt sores surfaced.

Was the diaper better than the bedpan?

By December 12, 2001, it took two people to move 80-pound Dad to a screaming, "God damn what are you doing to me now" sitting position.

The two people who moved Dad looked at me and explained that his butt sores were what was giving him pain. Dad's last meal was three small spoons of vanilla ice cream. He was in so much pain that he couldn't eat the ice cream. It actually had to run down his throat...so I quit feeding him. Dad died a half-hour after he was moved to that sitting position.

The Voodoo God said that a doctor should know that two surgeries on an 80-year-old man who never had a surgery in his life would kill him, which reminded me of my prayer: "may the murdered and the murderer remain together through all of eternity."

At the same moment, a few of the other Voodoo Gods were asking, "Was money involved?" Surgically removing bacterial infections was a bigger moneymaker than giving antibiotics when they were first needed.

All of a sudden God's vehicle appeared. I thought I heard God say: "The
next lie I hear you all say…you all will be minced meat pie!"

Instant Insanity
Chapter 32
Finders Fee

By January 2002, I had no doctor/drug prescriber because I asked too many questions. In order for me to receive an antibiotic, I have to have an expensive drug prescriber write me a prescription so that I can take the prescription to a drug store and pay additional money for the antibiotic prescription to be filled.

Many businesses gave what was called a "Finders Fee" when errors were discovered.

An example of a "Finders Fee" would be when I had gone to the grocery store to pick up Texas red grapefruit, green pea soup makings and a few other items. I looked at the Florida red grapefruit that were a bag of 6 for $1.99. The Texas ones were $1.00 each and didn't look as good. Then all I could find was yellow split peas. Immediately, I thought that this was going to be a bad shopping day, so I quit and walked to the checkout register. The two items totaled $3.78. I was over-charged a dollar. So, I walked back to re-read the $1.99 sign to make sure that I wasn't having a retard-moment. I decided that I would complain nicely, yet firmly...and get my dollar back.

The store employee and I walked to the grapefruit $1.99 sign. First the lady tried to tell me the $1.99 was for the bag that she was holding. "I wouldn't buy that one...look at the grapefruit!"

"Yuk," she said, "I wouldn't either." Again she rummaged through the grapefruit bags, and finally said, "Yes, that sign must be for all the bags here."

I followed her to the refund counter, where she filled out a "$5.00 Finder's Fee" slip plus my over-charged $1.00, so my refund was $6.00.

I'm changing the subject from grapefruit to blood tests. When I noticed that a blood test laboratory figure was raised 10 times what the figure should have been, there was no "Finder's fee".

Until a century ago, medicines and medical information was built on previously investigated history. An evil doctor would be like a medical terrorist. A medical lie would make a full circle, and when it reappeared the destruction would be devilish. This could show up in dreams such as Uncle Lewis's House where five metal stakes
appeared where a step should be.

The five metal stakes were explained in a previous dream. Betty's 1979 invisible medical book had presented three pages of lengthy medical disease study. The scurvy page had said two things: First was that a century ago, it was known that vitamin deficiency caused serious health problems and also invited infections. Second, it was known a century ago that the blood was used as a vehicle to transport nutrients and pathogens to the tissue.

Third was that most doctors knew about the evil doctor's curse and that the prescription drug law was designed to keep the 1908 tuberculosis vaccine from ever being used and to keep any tuberculosis vaccine from further development in the United States.

Fourth was at the time of the 1979 dream, doctors knew that antitumor/antiviral antibiotics were being withheld and discouraged from being further developed.

Stake number Five was at the time of the 1979 dream, a blood test called "Blood Typing Identification" was used by doctors to check blood before transfusion, yet by the 1990's lies were said that blood wasn't checked prior to transfusion.

A person should establish his/her personal blood test figure.

Again I use my husband's 1982 blood test as an example, which would be the 2-story drop. 1982 to 2002 equals 20. One story would be about 10 feet.

Carl's 1982 differential blood test was the following:

Test	Patients	Realist Figures	Lab's	Increased Figures
WBC	10.9H	4.8-10.0	4.8-10.8	

His personal figure was 6, which made the high figure extremely high.

Test	Patients	Realist Figures	Lab's	
Neutrophils	66*	54-62	45-75	
Lymphocytes	26	25-33	15-45	
Monocytes	6	3-7	0-12	
Eosinophils	1	1-3	0-4	
Basophils	1*	0-0.5	0-2.0	

The figures were not flagged because of laboratories increasing their figures four times what the Basophil figure should have been, therefore the cell abnormalities were not noticed. And again Carl received no antibiotics. Myelocytes used to be included in the white blood cell differential % figure. Myelocytes were found in the bone marrow and when they appeared in the blood, they were considered a disease marker.

Myelocytes and Basophils were stained together. Therefore the philosophy of "Closed eyes do not see".

I would not expect to go to a hematologist and have the hematologist claim that the blood means nothing!

Instant Insanity

Chapter 33

Deadly Situations

Evil doctors have been around since the invention of people. When the bloody-money talk would drip from the evildoer's lips, it was noticeable.

I knew it was a dream when I saw the spacey-saw-zaw in outer space. The colorful ringed object reminded me of the planet Saturn, only this object was without the planet. It was far enough away for me to view its full outline, yet close enough to hear its spinning roar...rummm-m...rumm-m.

The century old evil doctors curse: "I'll see you and your siblings sick before I see you receive the 1908 tuberculosis (TB) vaccine" lingers today. The curse had reached the point at which I noticed that I was deprived of my more effective antibiotics, and that I would never receive the TB vaccine.

Often as soon as a dream appeared the mirrored problem images would bring up a memory. In June 1996, my husband asked me to drive him to a local field so that he could crawl off to die like a dog. Carl was Gentimicin Sulfate USP drug over-dosed, as well as having two holes in his heart! It was illegal for me to drive Carl to a field to die, yet it wasn't illegal for blood test figures to be raised 10 times the normal figures…And the patient would be discouraged from establishing his/her personal blood test figure. That was a half-a-decade ago. The cardiologist, said, "You make it through this, it'll be like hitting a home run!" The cardiologist knew that the drug-of-choice on a 6-week protocol would drug-over-dose halfway through the recommended protocol.

I called the medical problem "A United States Enemy's Delight". In this same time slot, it was known that children's vaccines were being over-germed.

I believe that the same concerns would reappear in dream-themes. The dream would add something unfamiliar for the dreamer to investigate. Metal circle stampings had appeared on green grass prior to the dream titled "Uncle Lewis's House".

The dream:

A construction company first made the metal-circled-stamping imprints, then proceeded to dig up the ground, leaving an average house size foundation with a 2-story drop.

The huge hole was dug outside Uncle Lewis's house. The foundation was steep dirt. If you fell down the two-story drop, you would be unable to climb out. A second hole was where the first front step should have been. The house's step-size rectangular hole was made of poured cement. Five metal stakes the length of the 2-story deep step foundation were used to hold the step in place. Uncle Lewis's first step had been removed. The metal stakes were the length of the cement 2-story wall liner and were resting on the dirt ground below. The stakes were used to help hold the step in place. Whoever stepped out the door would probably plummet. I stood examining the missing step and the five metal rods. I wondered what kind of a construction company would charge for the unnecessary labor and material, and then leave the rest of the job undone, thereby endangering the homeowner.

I was standing outside, looking at the door, the missing step and the huge 2-story hole next to the missing step, when Uncle Lewis appeared. He had gone outside from a different door and walked around the house. When I saw him, I said, "I don't believe I see this!"

Uncle Lewis replied, "Yeah, that was pretty stupid of the builders. I can't believe they did this to me, either!"

We both looked at the cement step that was lying on the ground upside down. It was clear that the builders had deliberately moved the step. Whoever walked out would probably land on one of the five steel stakes. The dream scene examined the turned up-side-down cement step. There was a thick layer of clear spongy glue all along the outside edge.

The scene changed slightly. The house moved back. Uncle Lewis was standing where the house was, and I remained standing on the step's right side. We both were trying to replace the cement step so that whoever walked out wouldn't fall onto the steel spikes! The second large rectangular hole that was also a 2-story drop was next to the step, but it didn't have the steel spikes. Uncle Lewis said, "Get your husband to help me. The cement step is heavy!"

I was standing with one foot next to the edge. I could feel the dirt moving the pebbles over the side, as I replied, "Husband, too, is heavy and the ground next to the step is unstable…he'll fall down the second 2-story drop!"

The dream scene returned to the metal circle stampings that had appeared on the green grass surface. Each circle became magnified. The dream focused on one circle after another. I woke, thinking that I should write about the metal circle stampings.

End of Dream

The dream about the 2-story drop was clear. So during the day, my husband and I discussed June 27, 1996, the day when he asked me to drive him to a local field to drop him off like a dog, so that he could crawl off into a field to die. On June 28, 1996, the two medical specialists lied and prescribed a test that would have killed Carl. To make a long story short, Carl received a cadaver body part and lived. Never did the clinic give the cadaver's name. All that would have been five Christmases earlier, when we could say, "Thank you, cadaver person (name), for dying for us!"

The conversation ended with Carl saying, "You can tell me a lot of things…but don't tell me that God told you!"

It was very clear a half-decade ago that cardiologists knew that the recommendation would drug over-dose an endocarditis patient halfway through the recommended

6-week protocol. I called Medical Liars a United States Enemy's Delight a long time ago!

I concluded with a prayer for Adriamycin and Bleomycin, gram-negative antibiotics be given to the needy.

The Lord's Prayer

Our Father who art in heaven

hallowed by Thy name.

Thy kingdom come.

Thy will be done,

on earth, as it is in heaven.

Give us this day our daily bread,

and forgive us our trespasses

as we forgive those who trespass against us,

and lead us not into temptation,

but deliver us from evil.

For thine is the kingdom,

and the power, and the glory,

forever and ever.

Amen.